Guitar / Chords / Lyrics

In these silent days

Music transcriptions by Pete Billmann

ISBN 978-1-70514-635-4

Visit Hal Leonard Online at
www.halleonard.com

Contact us:
Hal Leonard
7777 West Bluemound Road
Milwaukee, WI 53213
Email: info@halleonard.com

In Europe, contact:
Hal Leonard Europe Limited
42 Wigmore Street
Marylebone, London, W1U 2RN
Email: info@halleonardeurope.com

In Australia, contact:
Hal Leonard Australia Pty. Ltd.
4 Lentara Court
Cheltenham, Victoria, 3192 Australia
Email: info@halleonard.com.au

Right On Time

Words and Music by Brandi Marie Carlile, Phillip John Hanseroth, Timothy Jay Hanseroth and Dave Cobb

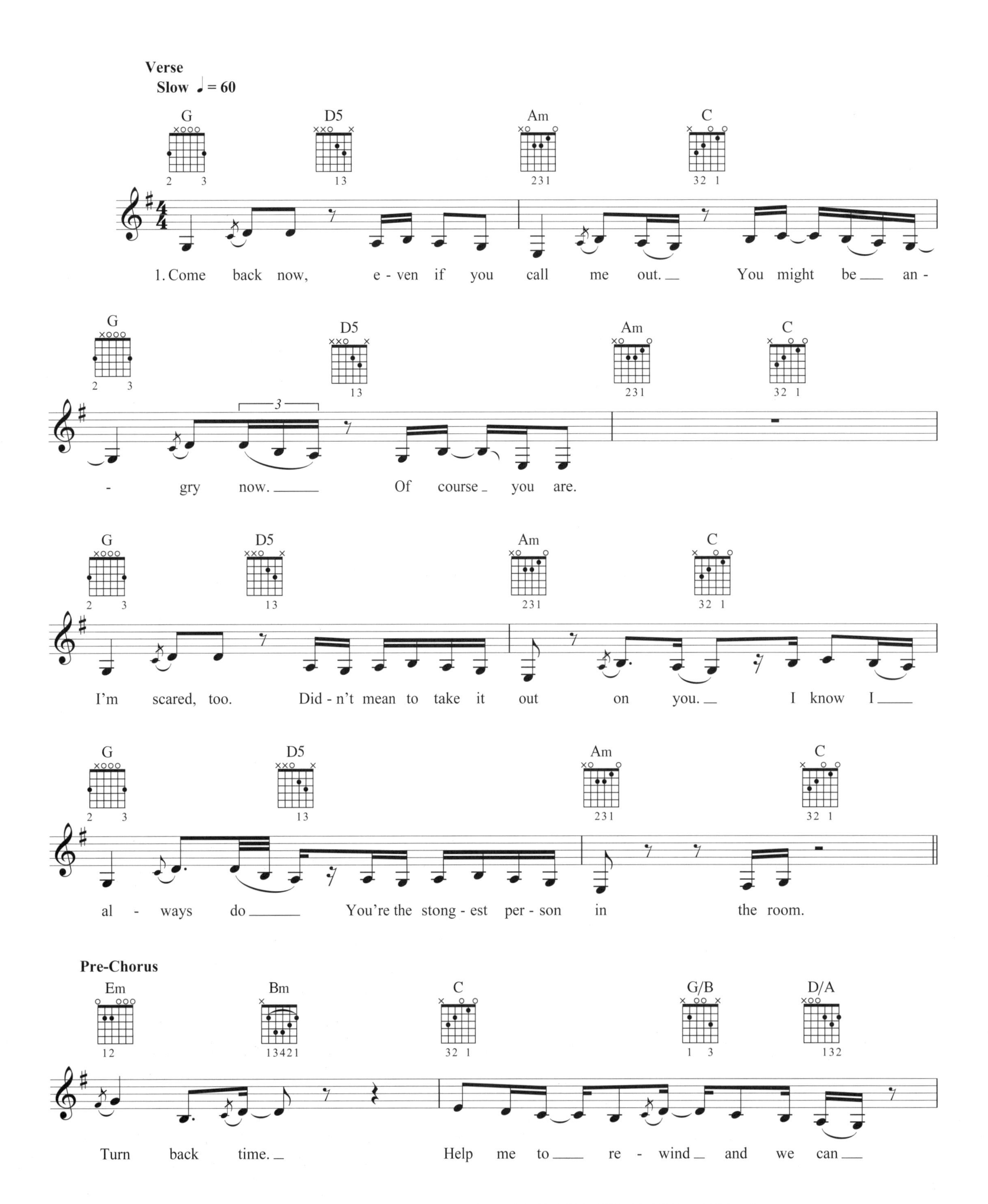

Em
Bm
D
D/C
find our - selves a - gain. It's not too late.
Chorus
G
G7
C
B7
Em
G
rit.
Ei - ther way, I lose you in these si - lent days. It was - n't right,
rubato
a tempo
D
D/C
G
Verse
G
D5
but it was right on time. 2. Don't look down. I can feel it when your
Am
C
G
D5
Am
C
heart starts pound - ing. It's be - yond your con - trol. You know it is. It's
G
D5
Em
C
get - ting to the point where I can't car - ry on. I nev - er held my breath for quite this
G
D5
Em
C
long. And I don't take it back, I did what I had to do. It's not too late.

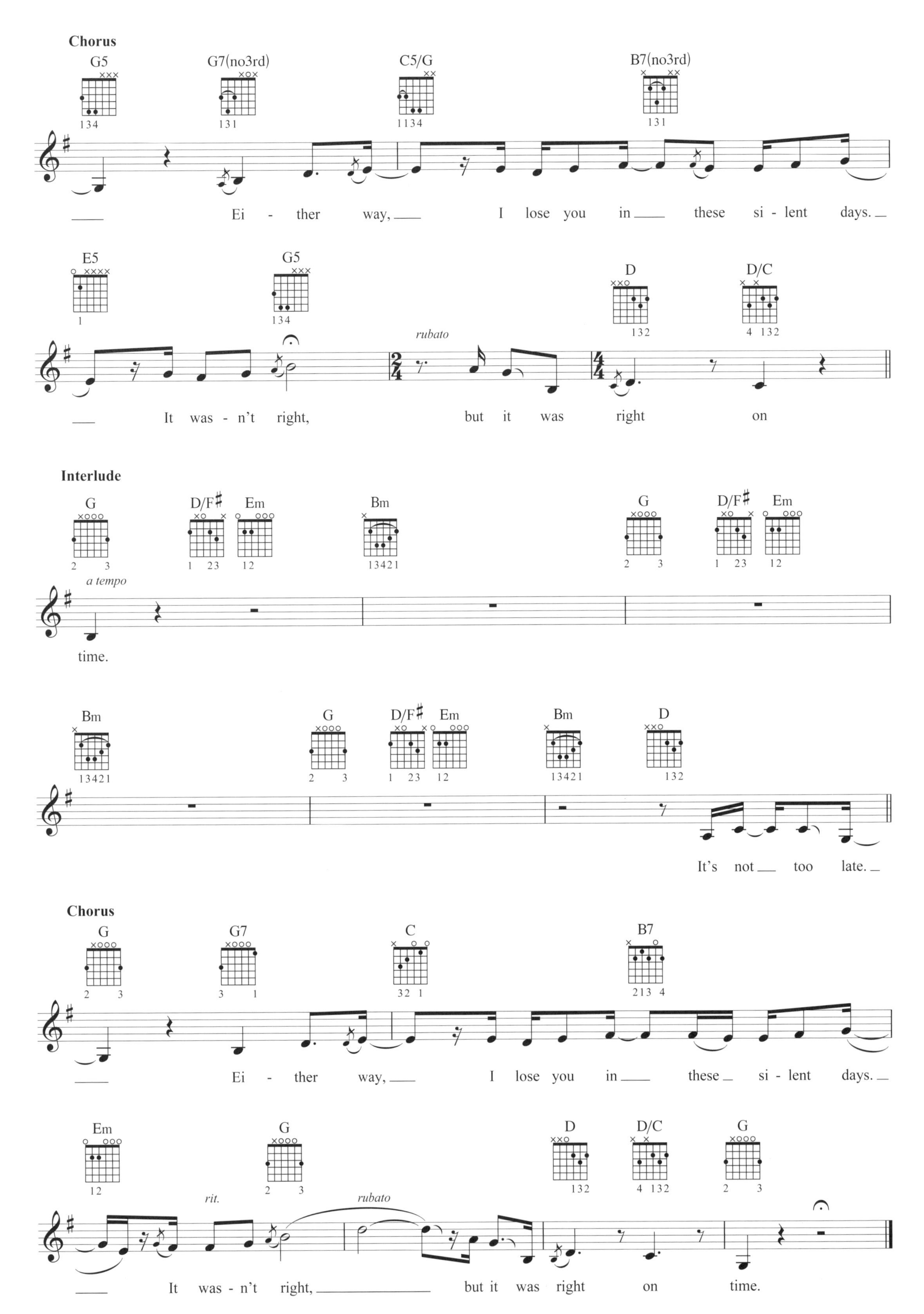
Chorus
G5 G7(no3rd) C5/G B7(no3rd)
Ei - ther way, I lose you in these si - lent days.
E5 G5 D D/C
rubato
It was - n't right, but it was right on
Interlude
G D/F♯ Em Bm G D/F♯ Em
a tempo
time.
Bm G D/F♯ Em Bm D
It's not too late.
Chorus
G G7 C B7
Ei - ther way, I lose you in these si - lent days.
Em G D D/C G
rit.
rubato
It was - n't right, but it was right on time.

You And Me On The Rock

Words and Music by Brandi Marie Carlile, Phillip John Hanseroth and Timothy Jay Hanseroth

Open D tuning, down 1/2 step:
(low to high) D♭-A♭-D♭-F-A♭-D♭

Intro

Moderately slow ♩ = 86

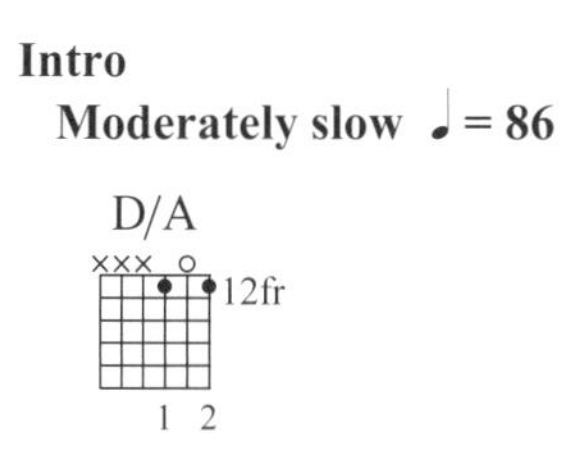

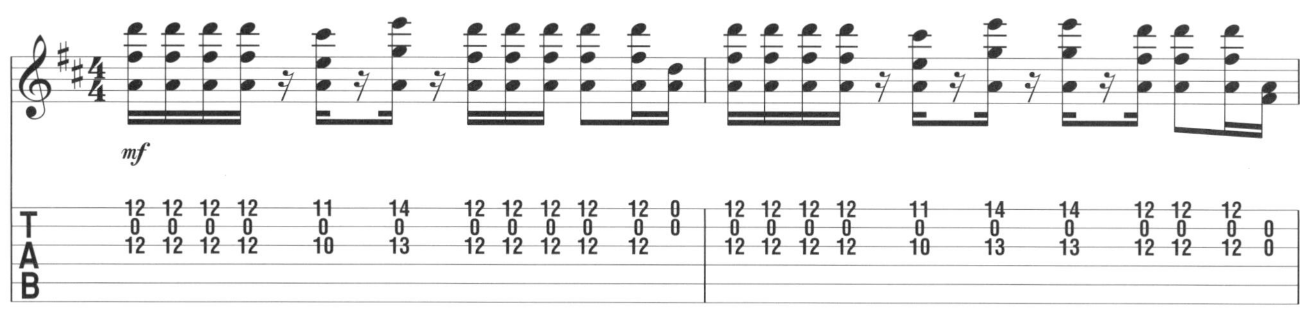

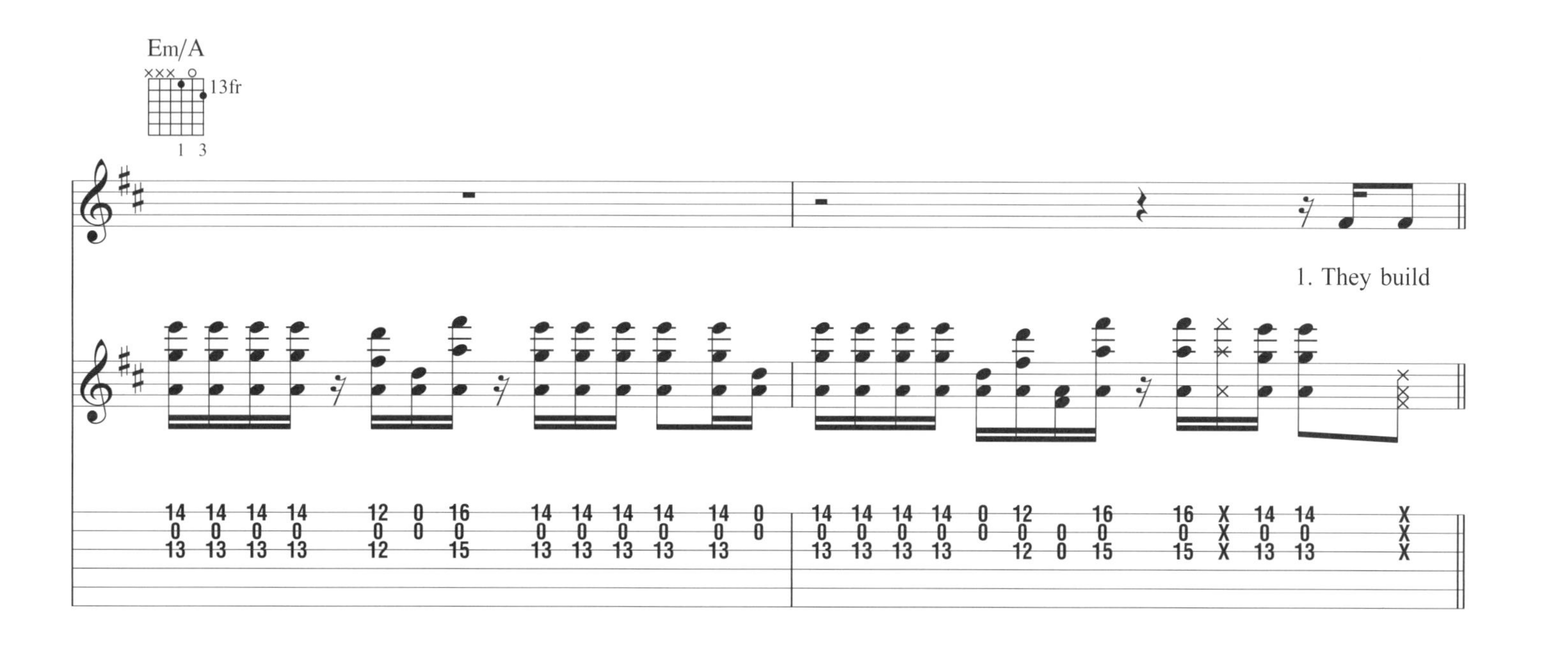

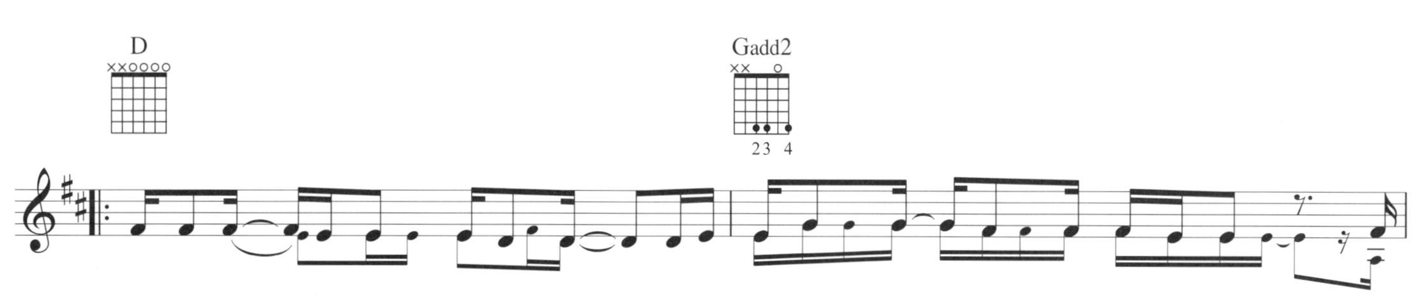

D
ag - o - nal lines in their rolled - out lawns and the sage al - ways smells so pret - ty. But
fold - ed them crook - ed and now I'm won-der-ing why I could al - ways end up in the wa-ter.

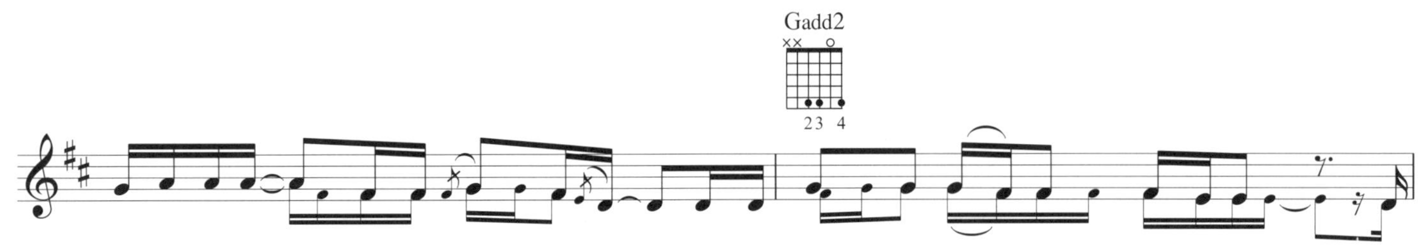
Gadd2
23 4
no-bod - y cares where the birds have gone when the rain comes down on Bab - y- lon. The
No-bod-y's ask - ing why she look-ing so thin, why she's laugh-ing too hard, why she's drink-ing a - gain. A

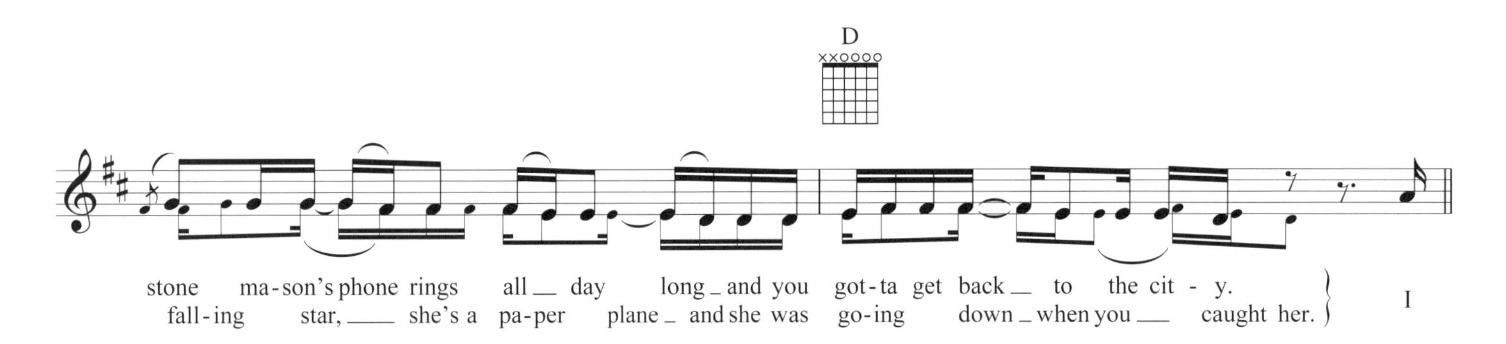
D
stone ma-son's phone rings all day long and you got-ta get back to the cit - y.
fall-ing star, she's a pa-per plane and she was go-ing down when you caught her.
I

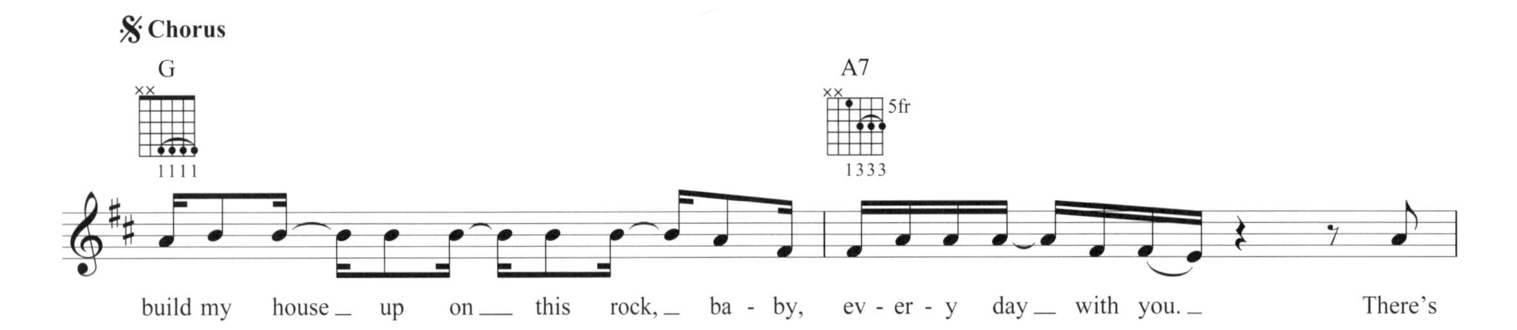
Chorus
G
1111
A7
5fr
1333
build my house up on this rock, ba - by, ev - er - y day with you. There's

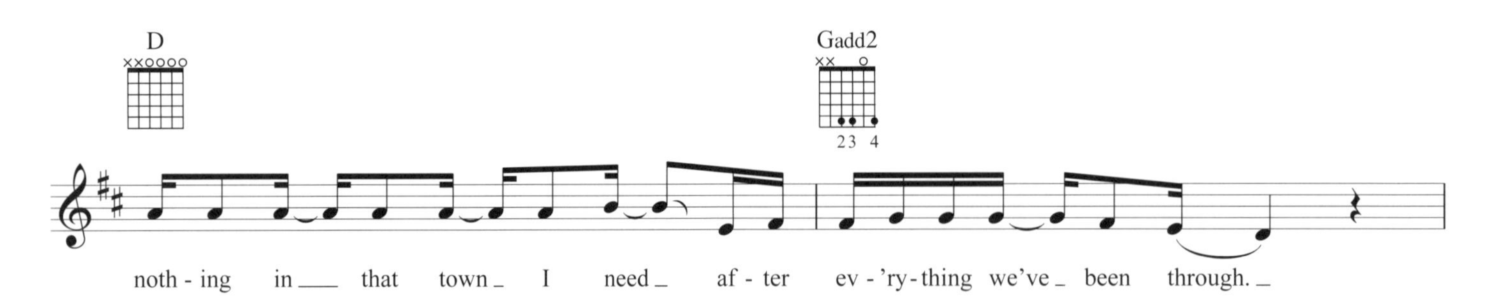
D
Gadd2
23 4
noth - ing in that town I need af - ter ev - 'ry-thing we've been through.

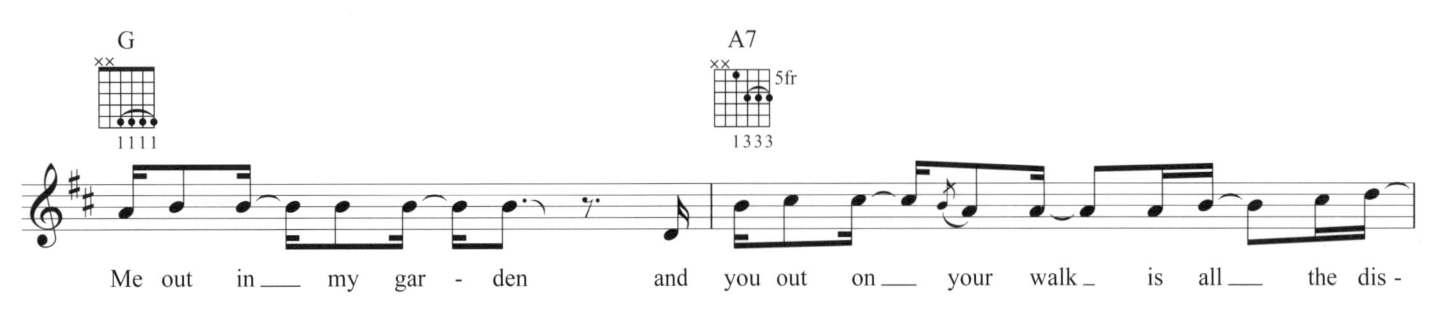
G
1111
A7
5fr
1333
Me out in my gar - den and you out on your walk is all the dis -

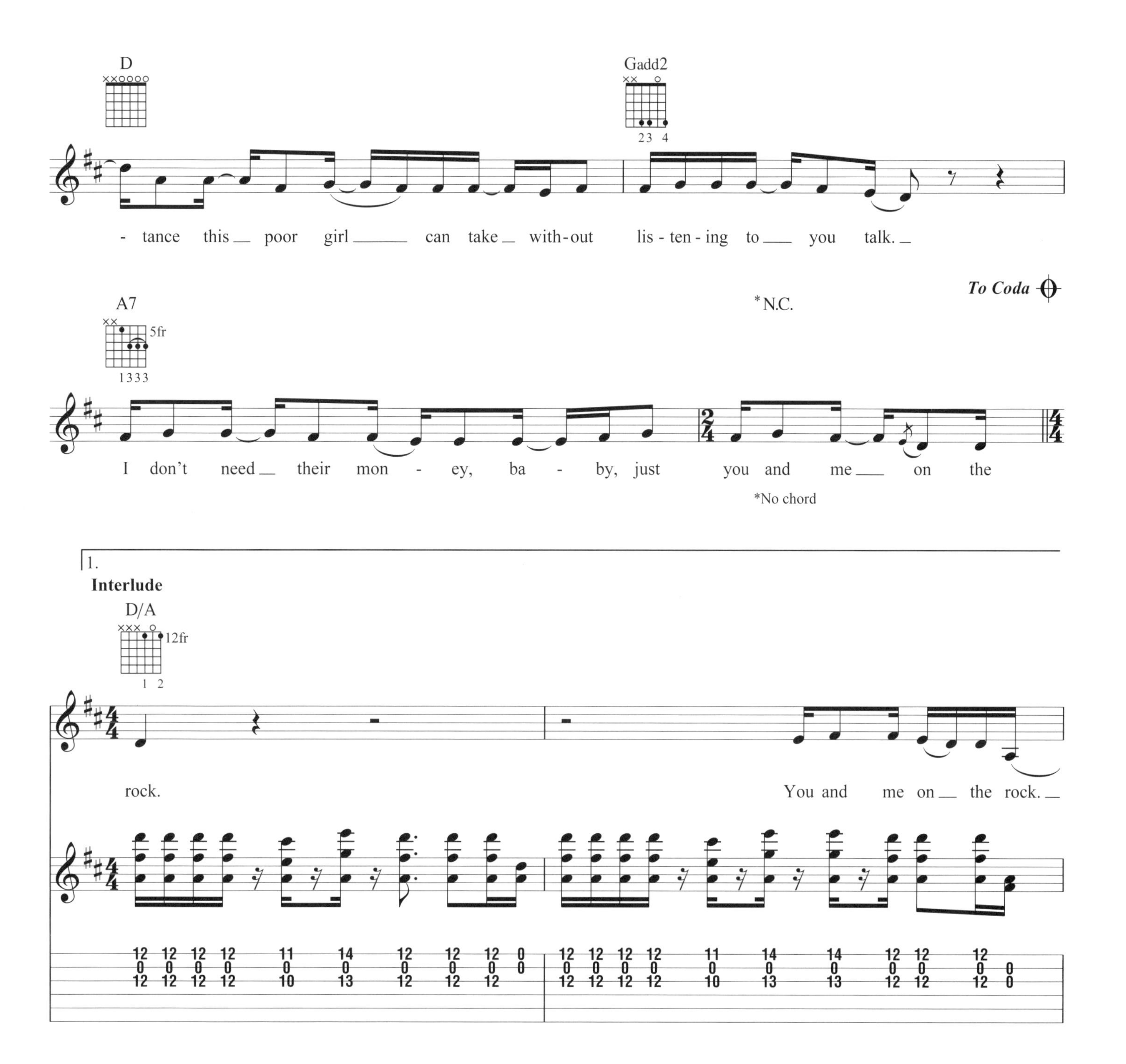

D
Gadd2
23 4
- tance this poor girl can take with-out lis-ten-ing to you talk.
To Coda
A7
5fr
1333
*N.C.
I don't need their mon - ey, ba - by, just you and me on the
*No chord
1.
Interlude
D/A
12fr
1 2
rock. You and me on the rock.

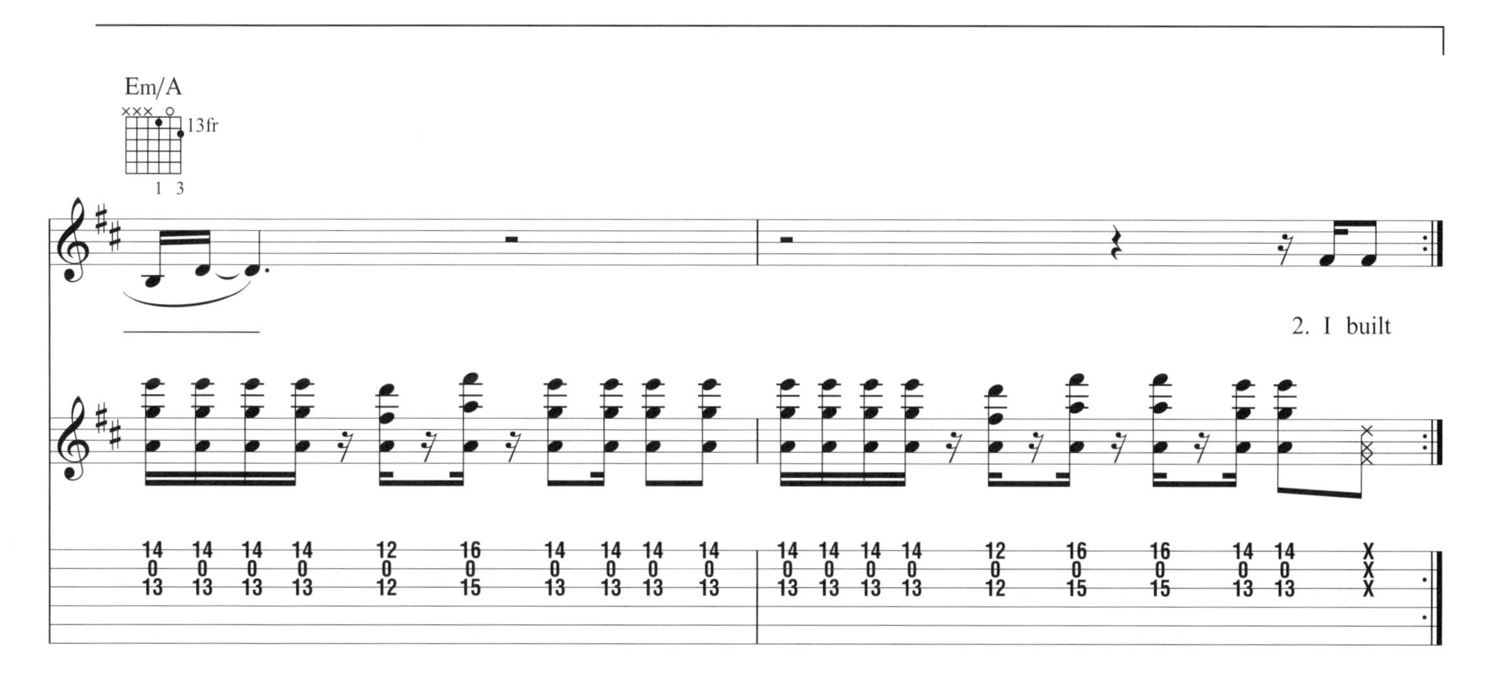

Em/A
13fr
1 3
2. I built

2.
D
rock.
It's an earth-
Bridge
Csus4
5fr
1241
G
1111
- quake,
it's a hard
wind.
It's a
D
A
7fr
1111
Asus4
7fr
1211
re - cord - break - ing tide and it is roll - ing in.
It's a big
Csus4
5fr
1241
G
1111
sea,
but it can't touch you and me.
It's just a wa - ter
A
7fr
1111
Asus4
7fr
1211
A
7fr
1111
view,
and what a view.

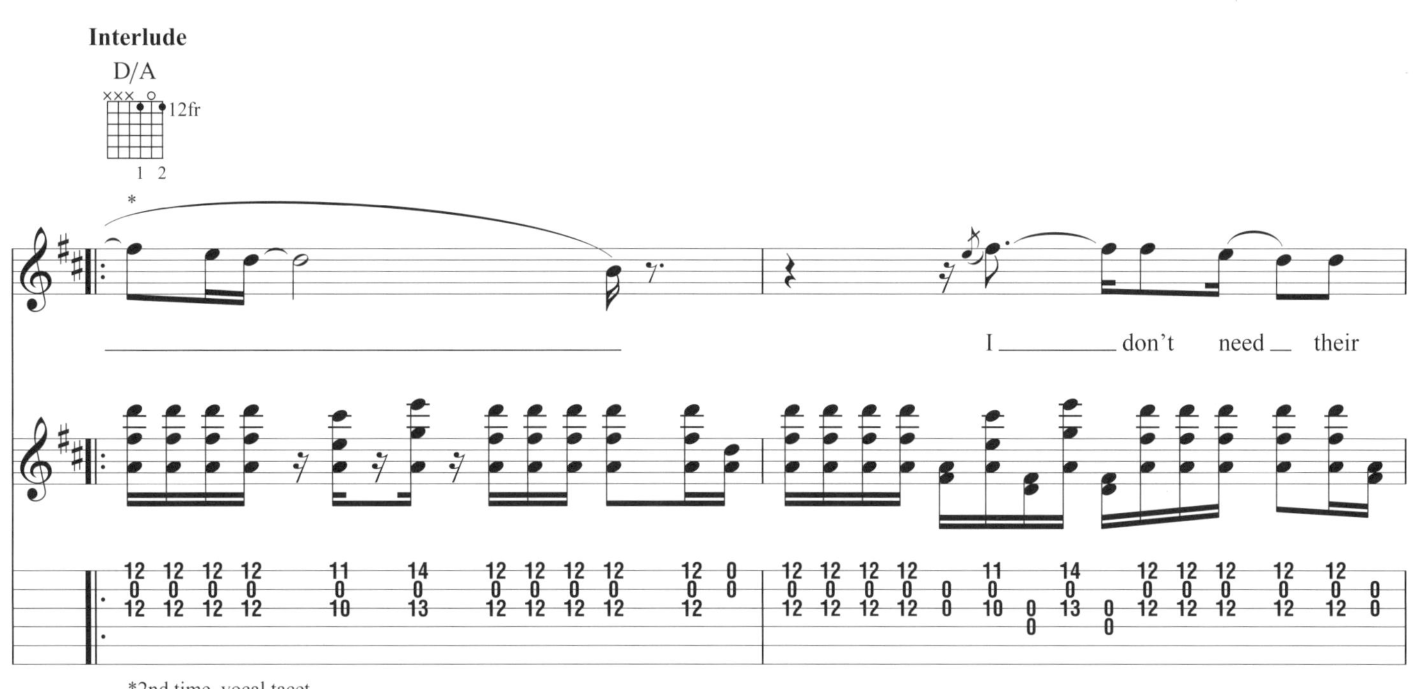

*2nd time, vocal tacet

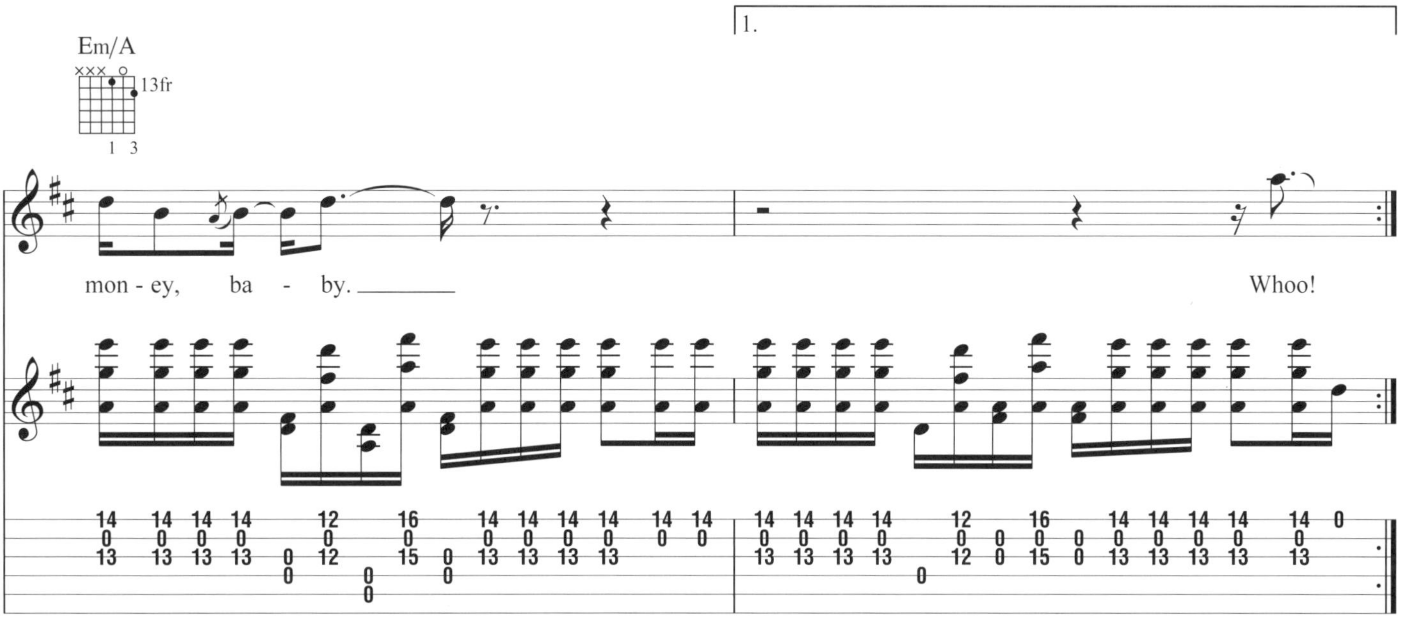

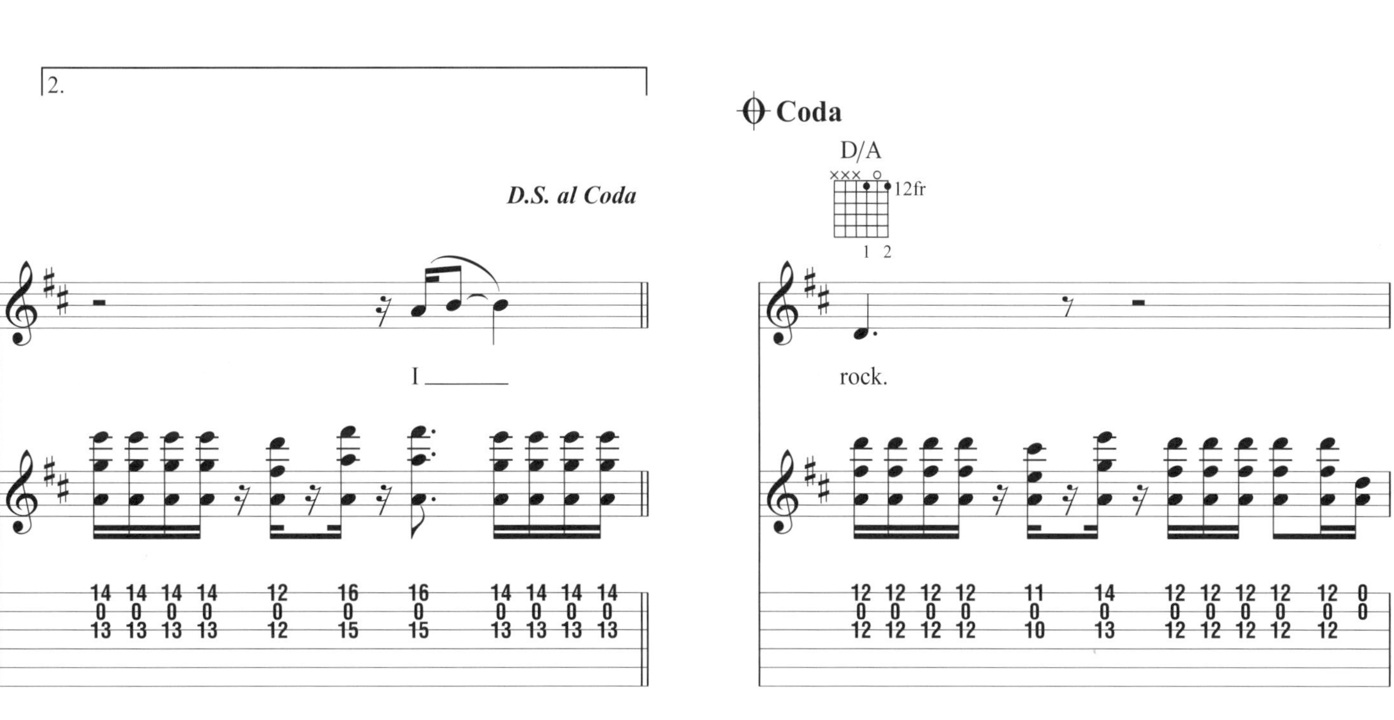

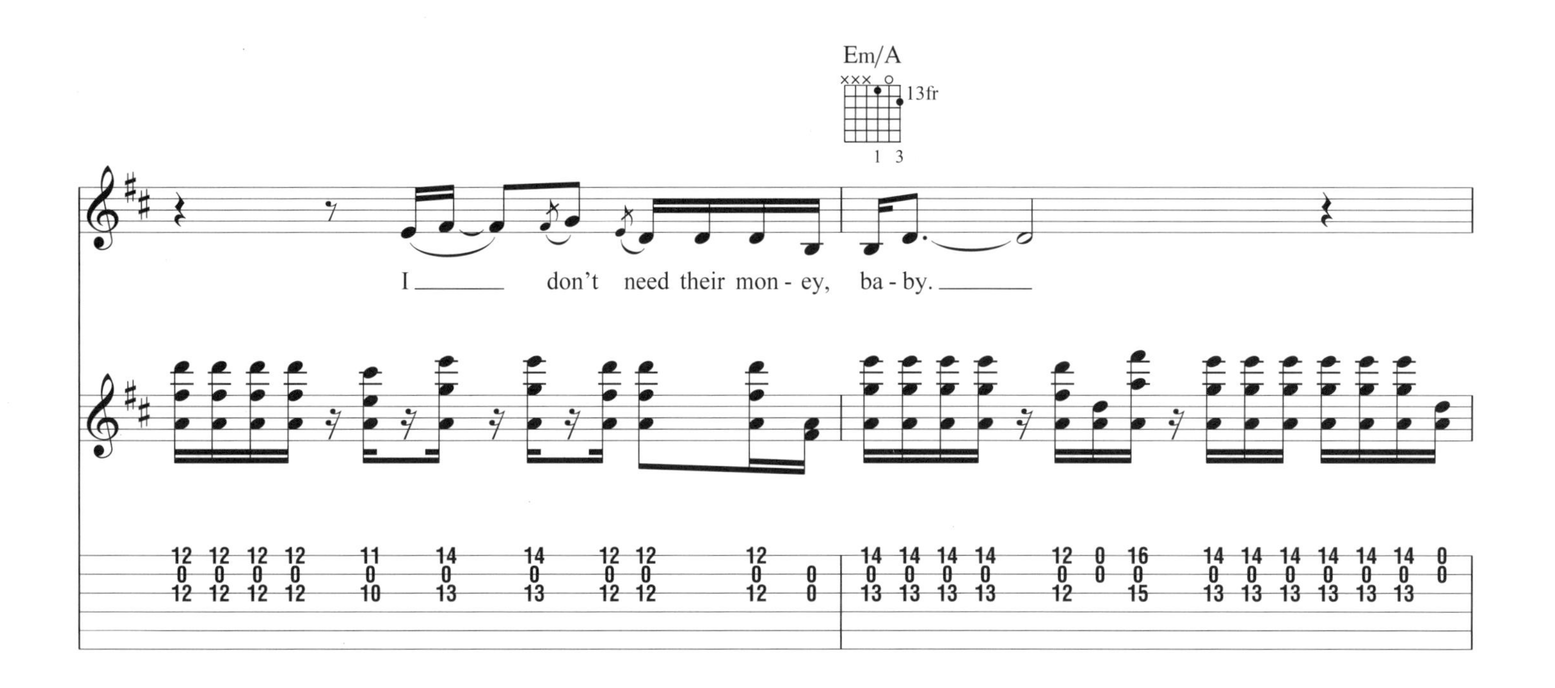
Em/A
13fr
1 3
I don't need their mon-ey, ba-by.
12 12 12 12 11 14 14 12 12 12
0 0 0 0 0 0 0 0 0 0 0
12 12 12 12 10 13 13 12 12 12 0
14 14 14 14 12 0 16 14 14 14 14 14 14 0
0 0 0 0 0 0 0 0 0 0 0 0 0 0
13 13 13 13 12 15 13 13 13 13 13 13

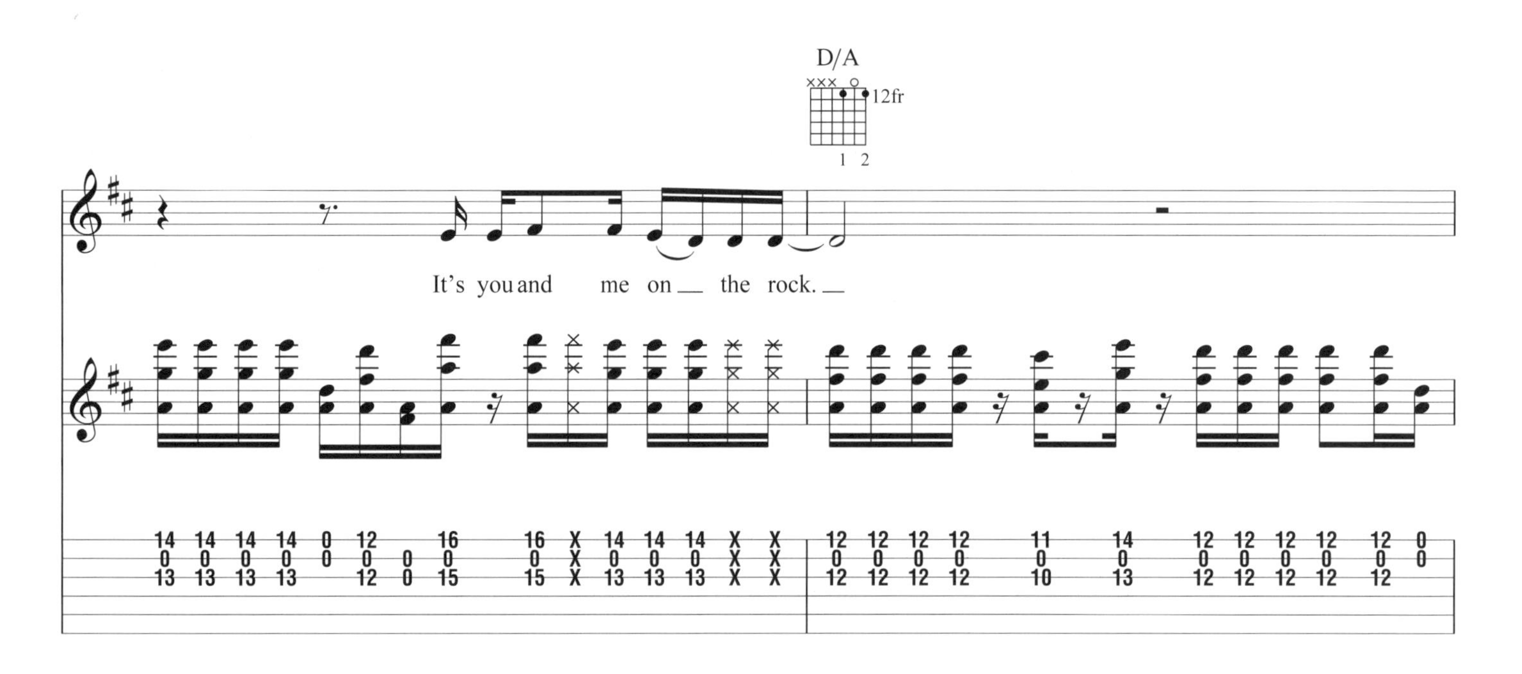
D/A
12fr
1 2
It's you and me on the rock.
14 14 14 14 0 12 16 16 X 14 14 14 X X
0 0 0 0 0 0 0 0 0 X 0 0 0 X X
13 13 13 13 12 0 15 15 X 13 13 13 X X
12 12 12 12 11 14 12 12 12 12 12 0
0 0 0 0 0 0 0 0 0 0 0 0
12 12 12 12 10 13 12 12 12 12 12

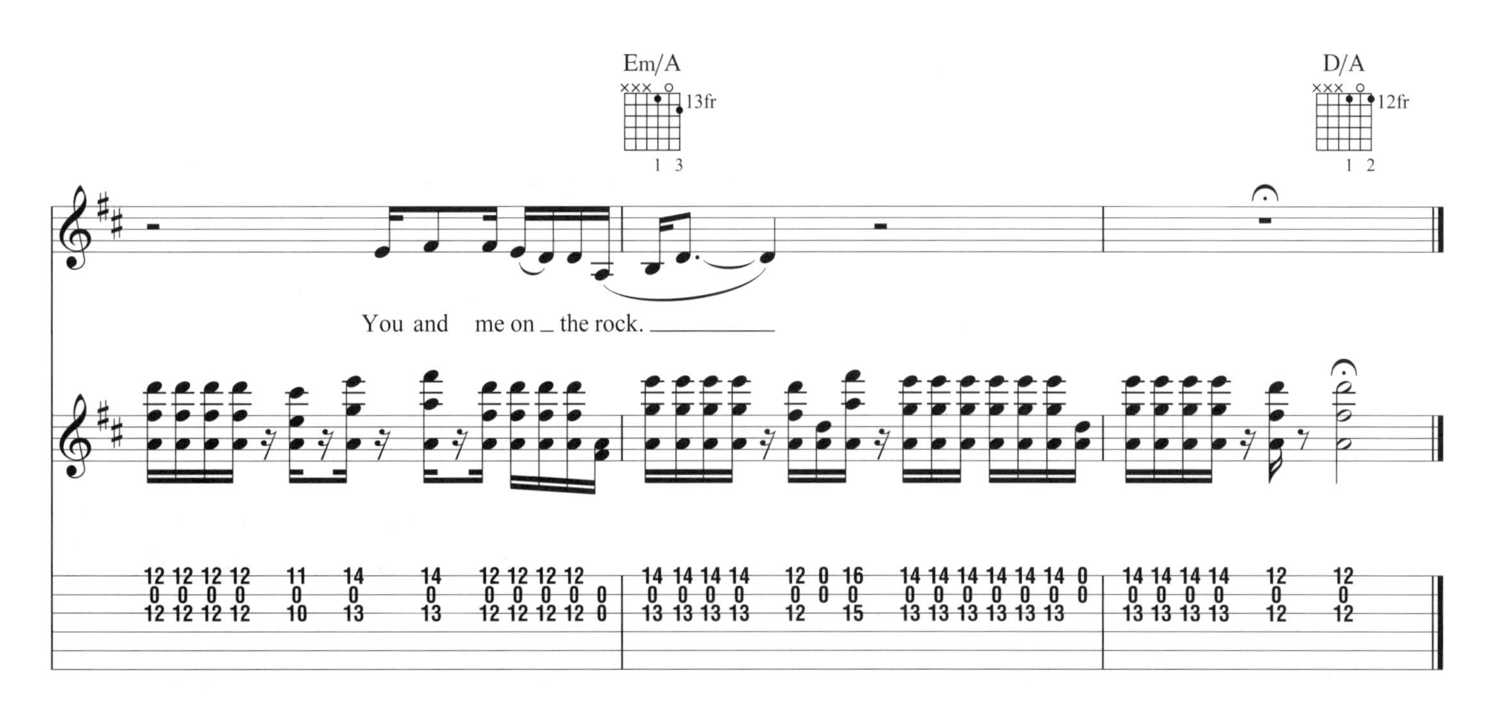
Em/A
13fr
1 3
D/A
12fr
1 2
You and me on the rock.
12 12 12 12 11 14 14 12 12 12 12
0 0 0 0 0 0 0 0 0 0 0 0
12 12 12 12 10 13 13 12 12 12 12 0
14 14 14 14 12 0 16 14 14 14 14 14 14 0
0 0 0 0 0 0 0 0 0 0 0 0 0 0
13 13 13 13 12 15 13 13 13 13 13 13
14 14 14 14 12 12
0 0 0 0 0 0
13 13 13 13 12 12

This Time Tomorrow

Words and Music by Brandi Marie Carlile, Phillip John Hanseroth and Timothy Jay Hanseroth

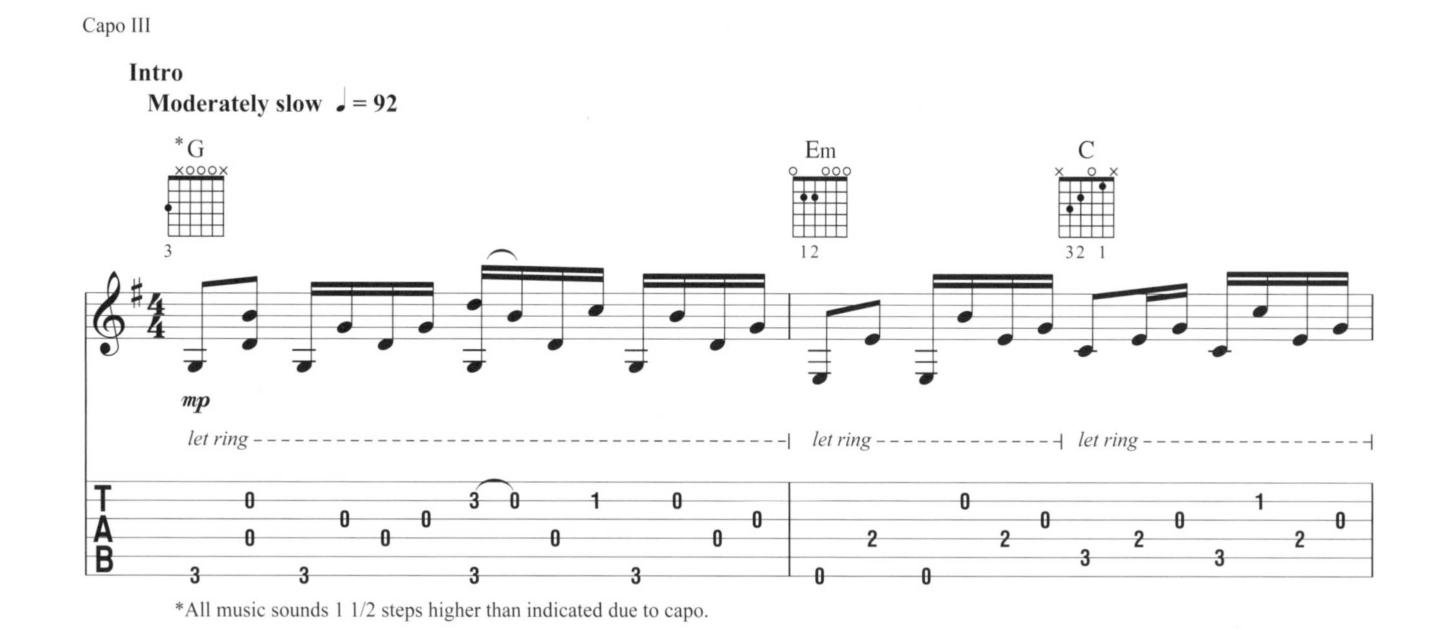

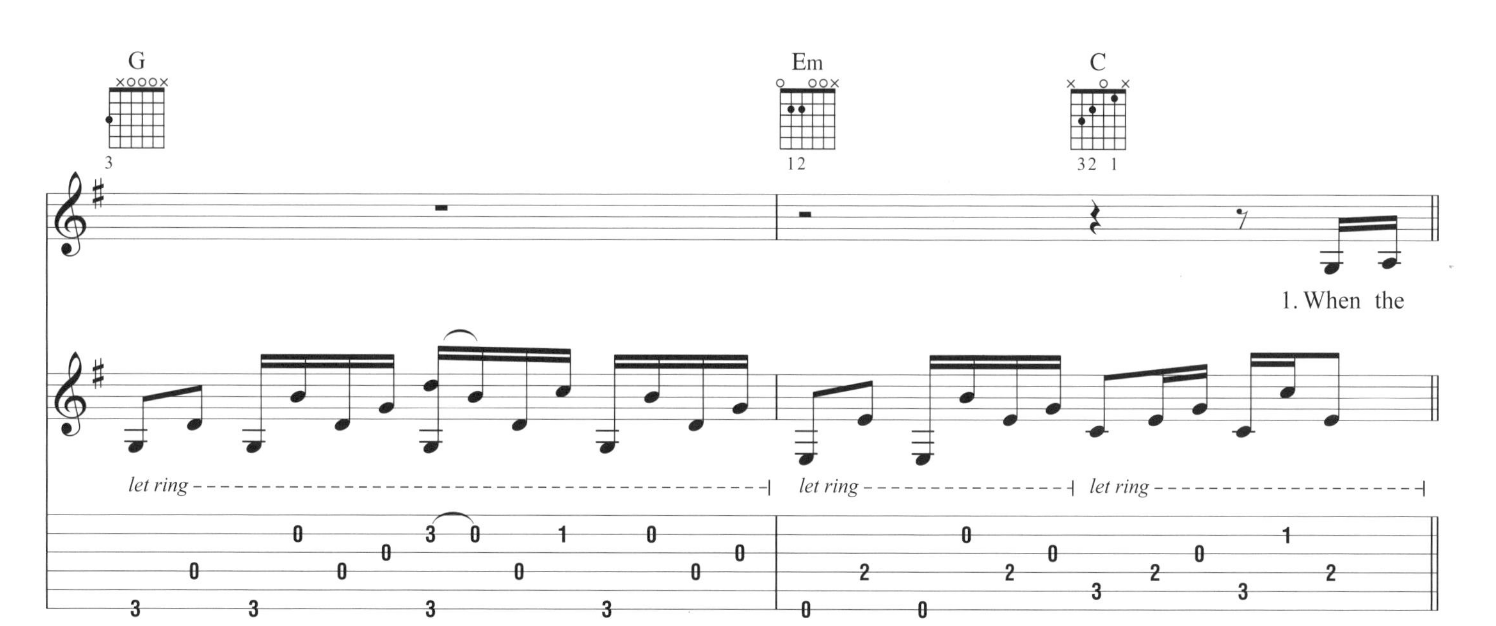

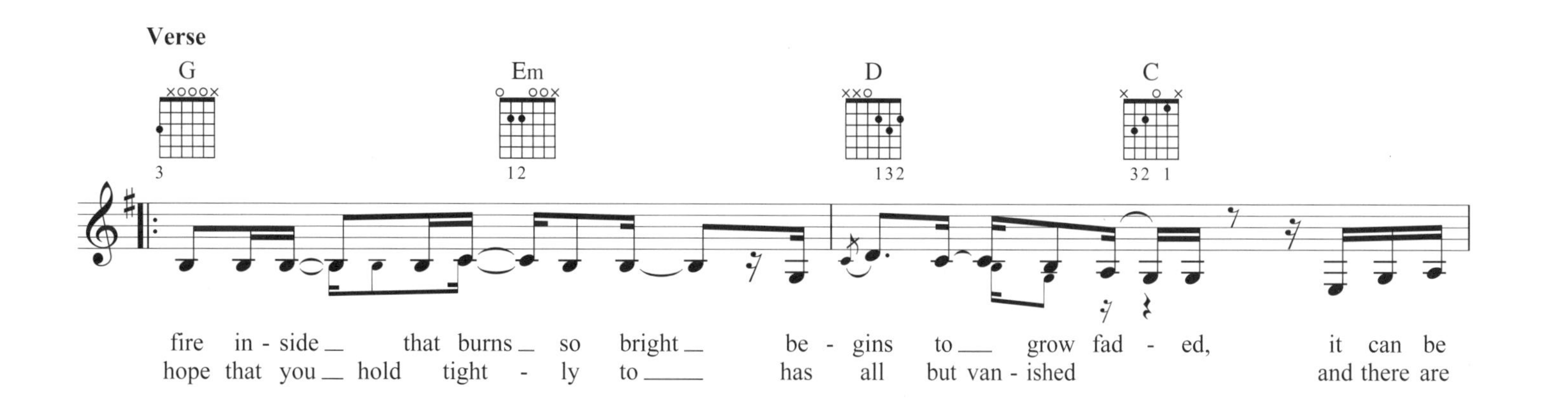

G
Em
Bm
hard to see the ground on which you stand. Though you
no words of com - fort to be found, you will
C
G
may not be a - fraid of walk - ing in the dark - ness, you will
know what it means to be lost and with - out love. May you
D
Em
feel like a strang - er in this land. You can
fight to kill that deaf - en - ing sound. But our
Chorus
C
C/B
Am7
G
D/F#
(1., 3.) try to carve a faith out of your own, but a
(2.) ho - ly dreams of yes - ter - day aren't gone. They still haunt
let ring
G
C
bro - ken spir - it may dry out the bone. And the
us like the ghosts of Bab - y - lon. And the

C/B
Am7
G
D/F♯
ed - ges of the night may cause you sor - row.
break - ing of the day might bring you sor - row,
You know I
To Coda
C
D5/A
may not be a - round this time to - mor - row,
but I'll al - ways be with
Interlude
Em
you.
Yeah,
I'll,
I'll al - ways be with you.
let ring
1.
2.
2. When the

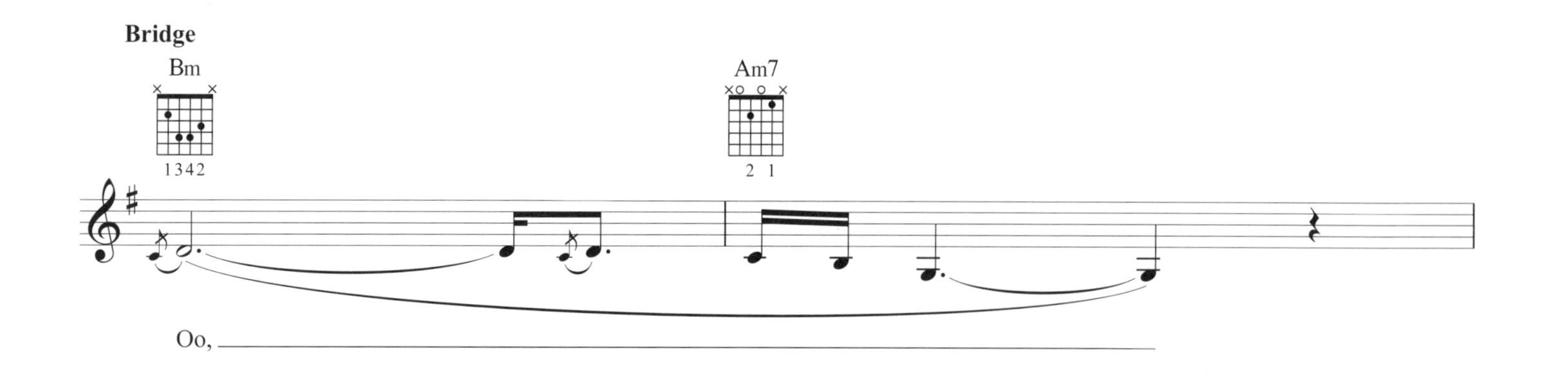

Bridge
Bm
1342
Am7
2 1
Oo,

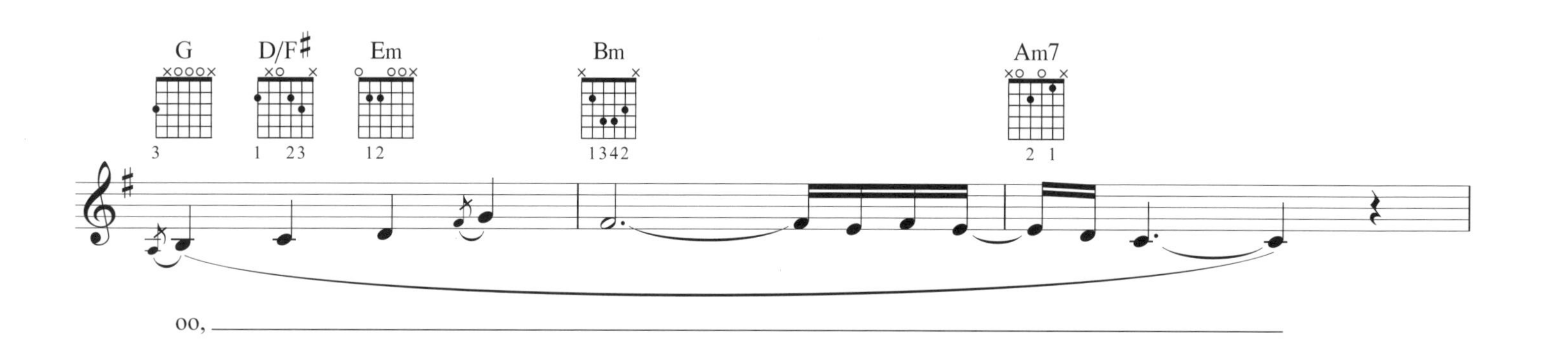

G
3
D/F♯
1 23
Em
12
Bm
1342
Am7
2 1
oo,

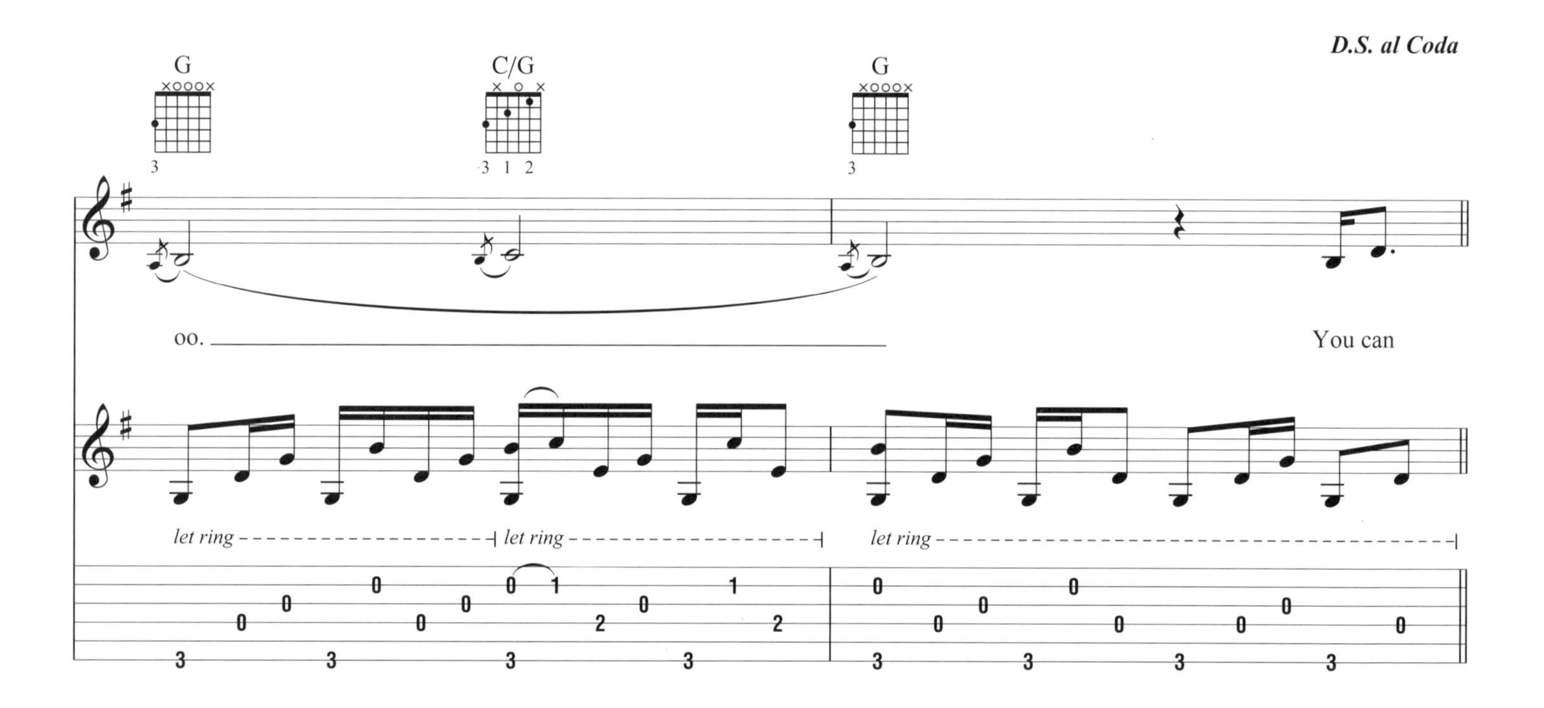

D.S. al Coda
G
3
C/G
3 1 2
G
3
oo.
You can
let ring
let ring
let ring

Coda
C
32 1
C/B
2 1
Am7
2 1
G
3
mor - row.
But our
ho - ly dreams
of yes - ter - day
aren't

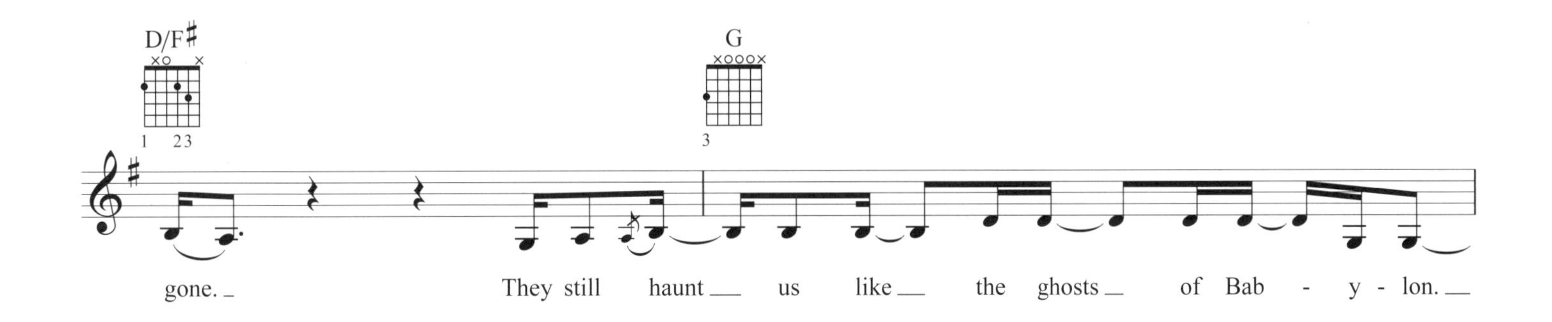
D/F#
G
gone. _ They still haunt __ us like __ the ghosts _ of Bab - y - lon. __

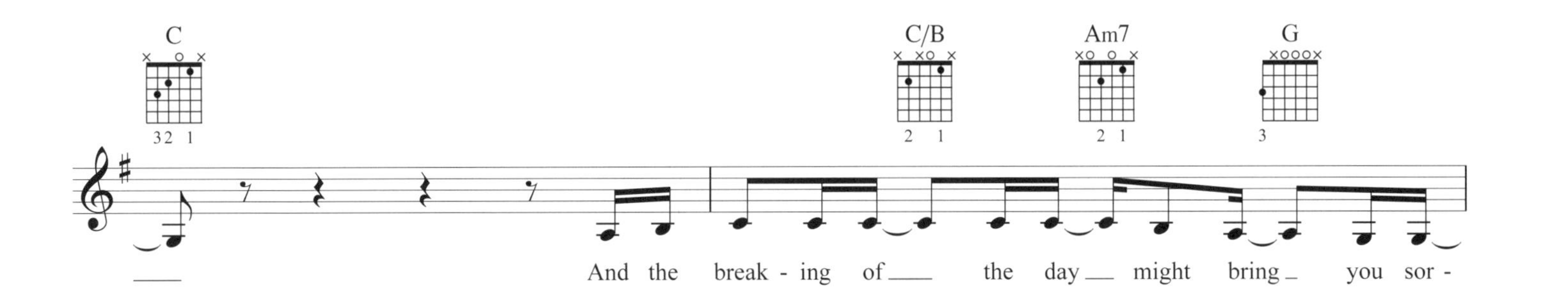
C
C/B
Am7
G
And the break - ing of __ the day __ might bring _ you sor -

D/F#
G
C
- row. You know I may not be a - round _ this time _ to - mor - row, ____

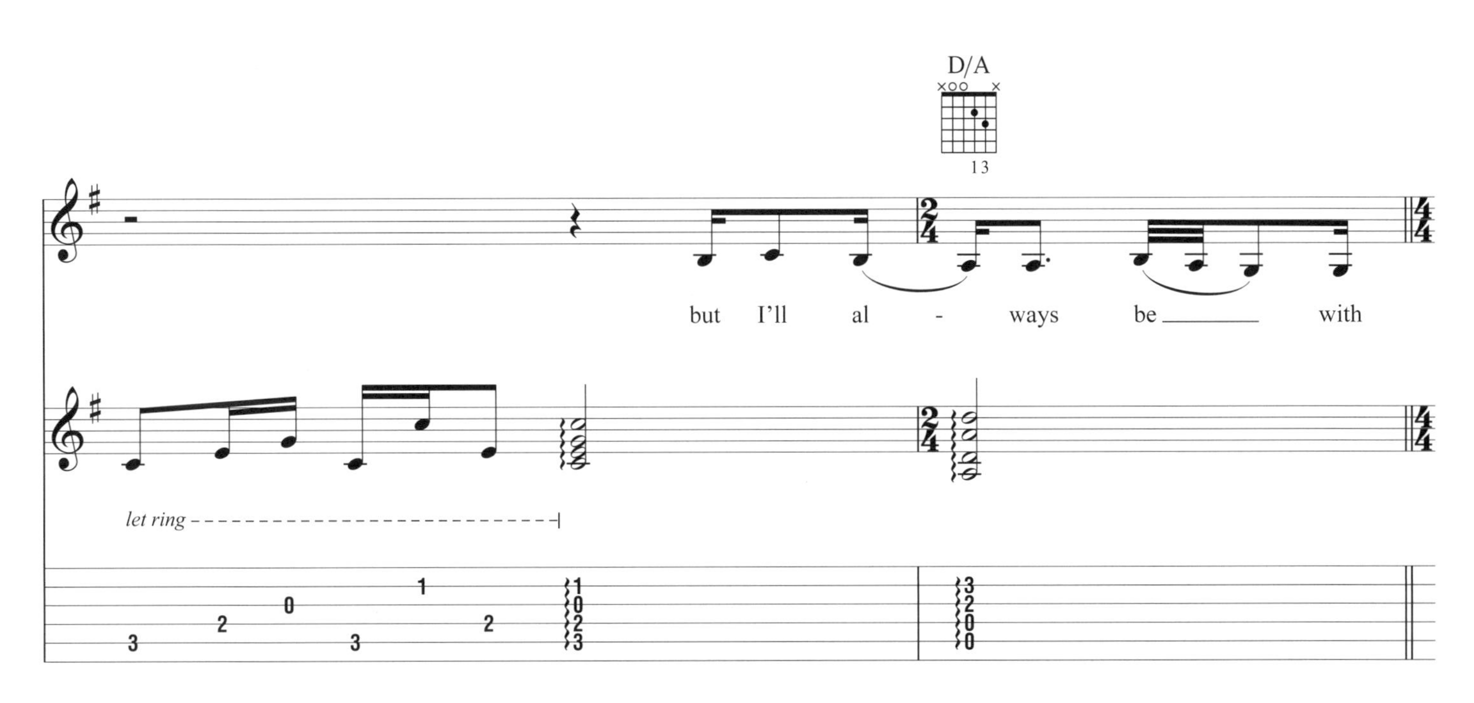
D/A
but I'll al - ways be ____ with
let ring

Outro
G
Em
C
you.
I will al - ways be with you.
let ring
G
Em
C
I will al - ways be with you.
let ring
G
Em
C
G
rit.
I'll al - ways be with you.
let ring
rit.

Broken Horses

Words and Music by Brandi Marie Carlile, Phillip John Hanseroth and Timothy Jay Hanseroth

Drop D tuning:
(low to high) D-A-D-G-B-E

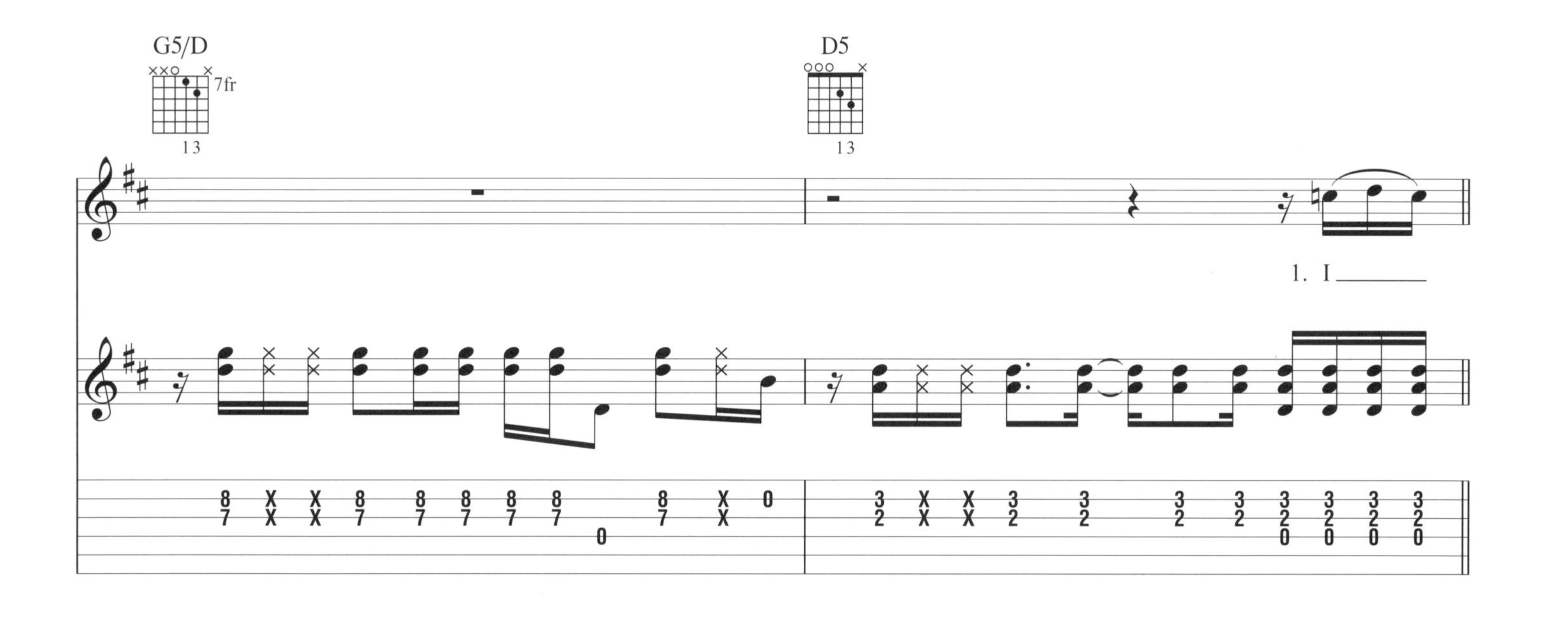

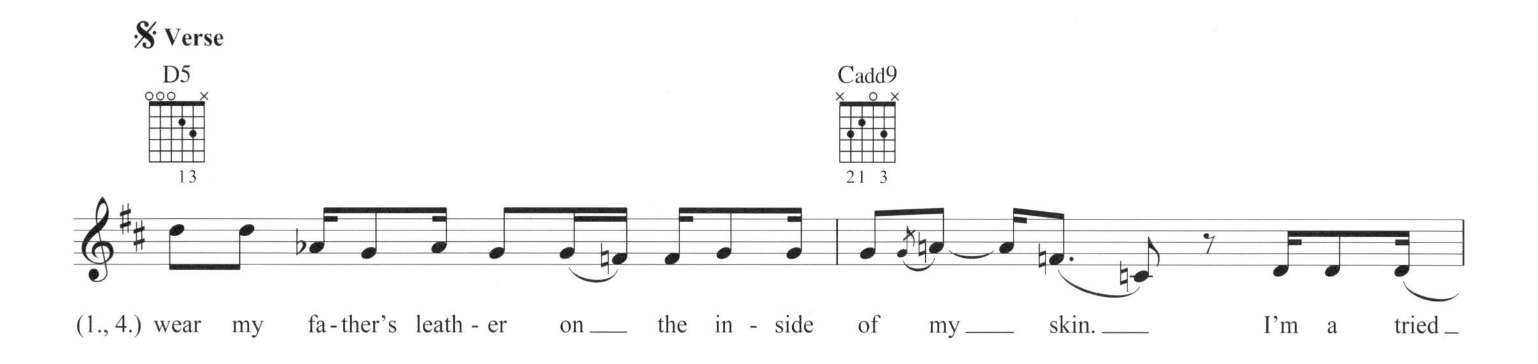

F6/9(no3rd)
F
C
and weath - ered wom - an, but I won't be tried a - gain. Don't
D5
Cadd9
think that you can come for me with - out your Sun - day best. You had
bet - ter call your priest and hope the dev - il gets the rest be - fore I do.
To Coda 1
D
F/D
G/D
D
Aw, and I will do.
2. I've
worn the jest - ter's bells and I have ban - ished with the fools. I have
ev - er so po - lite - ly tread - ed soft - ly for your grace. I have
wor - shipped at the al - tar of the pup - pet mas - ter's rules. I have
whis - pered through the tears and plead - ed sweet - ly to your face. It is

D
C
held my tongue too man-y scenes be-fore the fi-nal act with my
time to spit you out like luke-warm wa-ter from my mouth. I will
F
C
chil-dren in the cheap seats and a zip-per on my back thanks to you.
al-ways taste the ap-a-thy, but I won't pass it down. It dies
D
F/D
No thanks to you.
with you,
you.
G/D
D
Chorus
D
F
G9
Teth-ered in wide o-pen spac-es and fields that lead for miles,

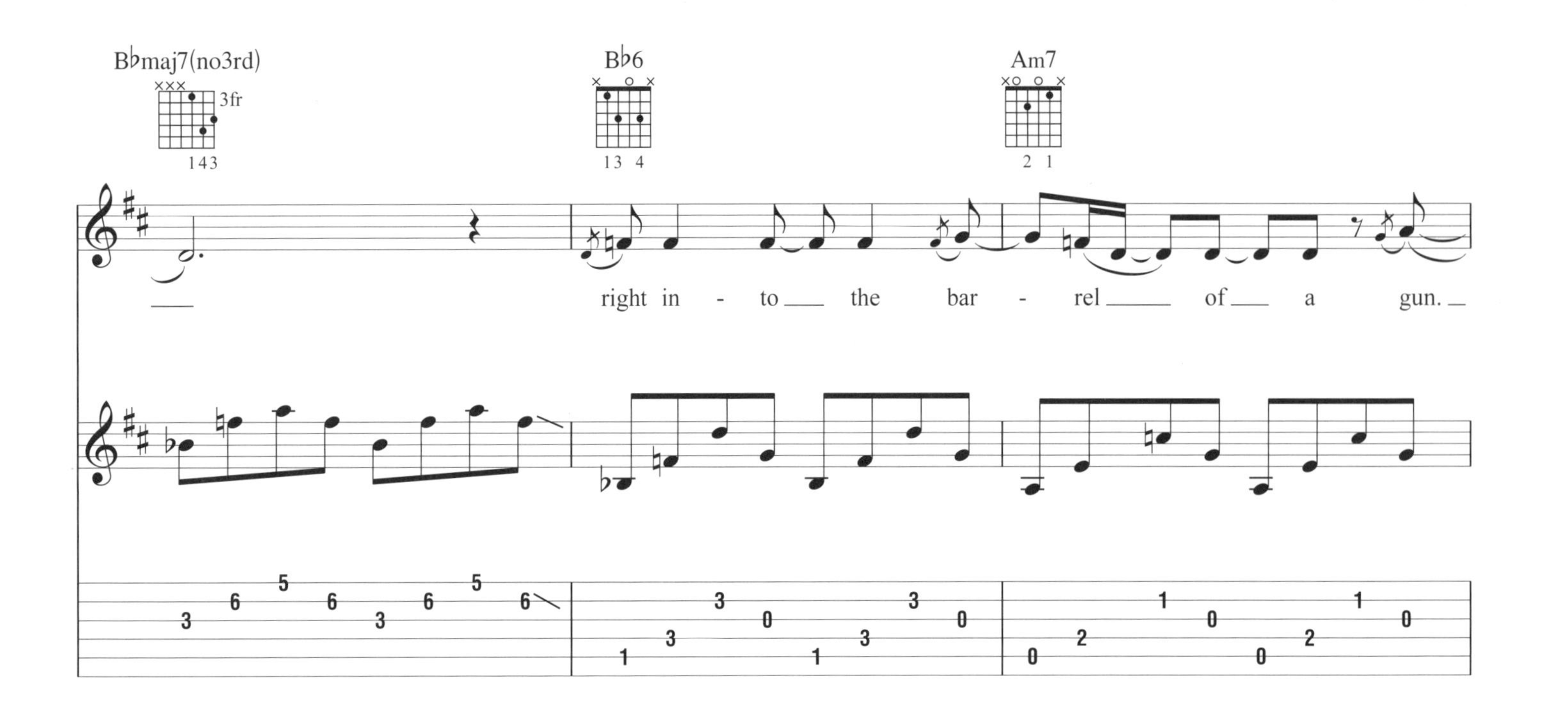

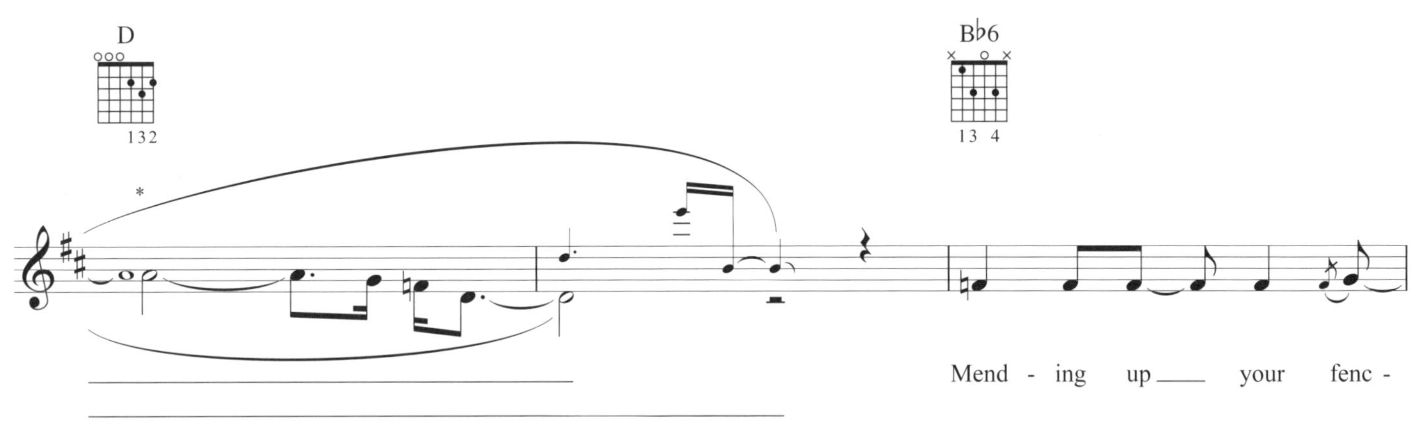

*3rd time, sing vocal cues
extender for cue part

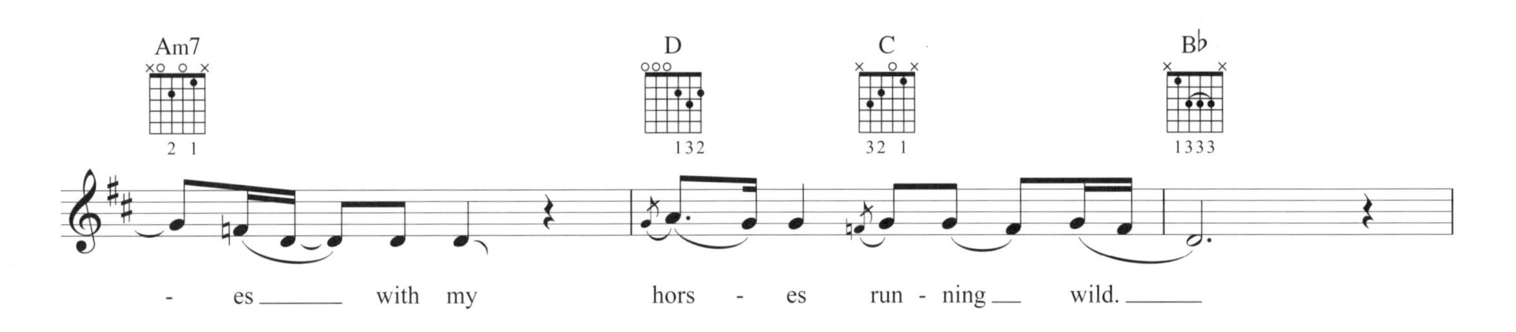

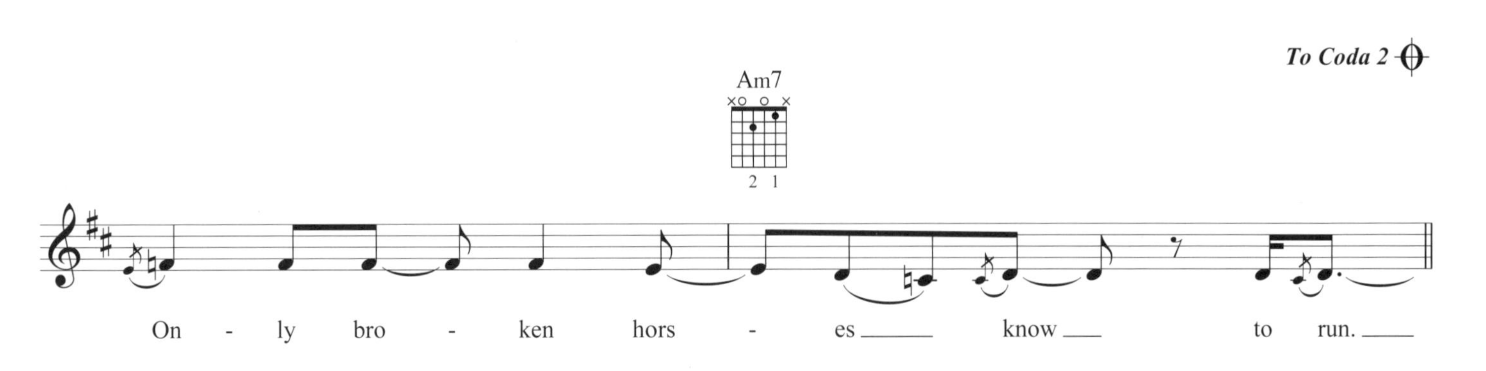

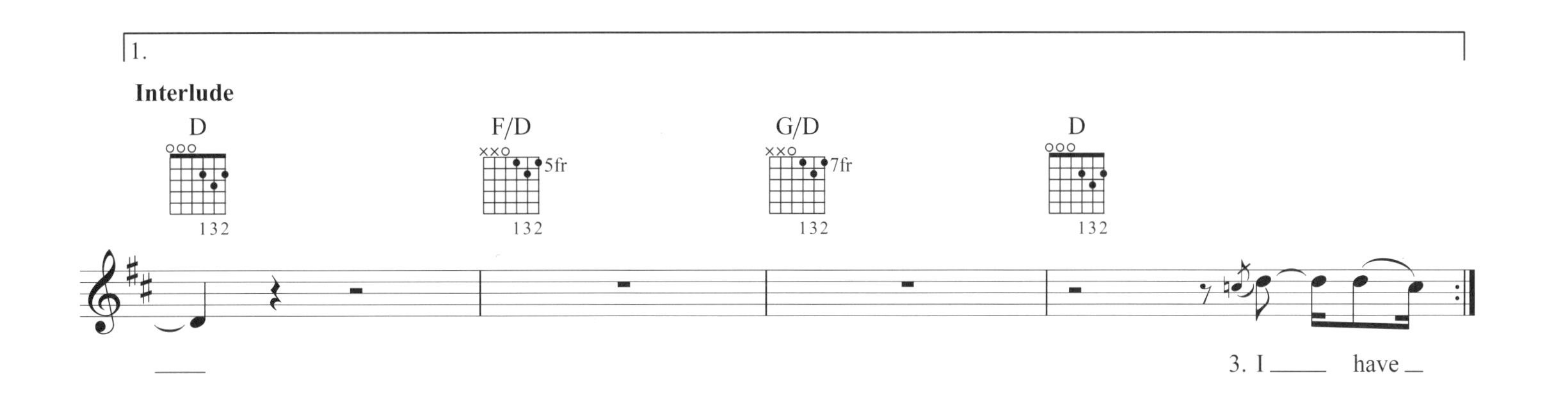
1.
Interlude
D
F/D
5fr
G/D
7fr
D
3. I ___ have ___

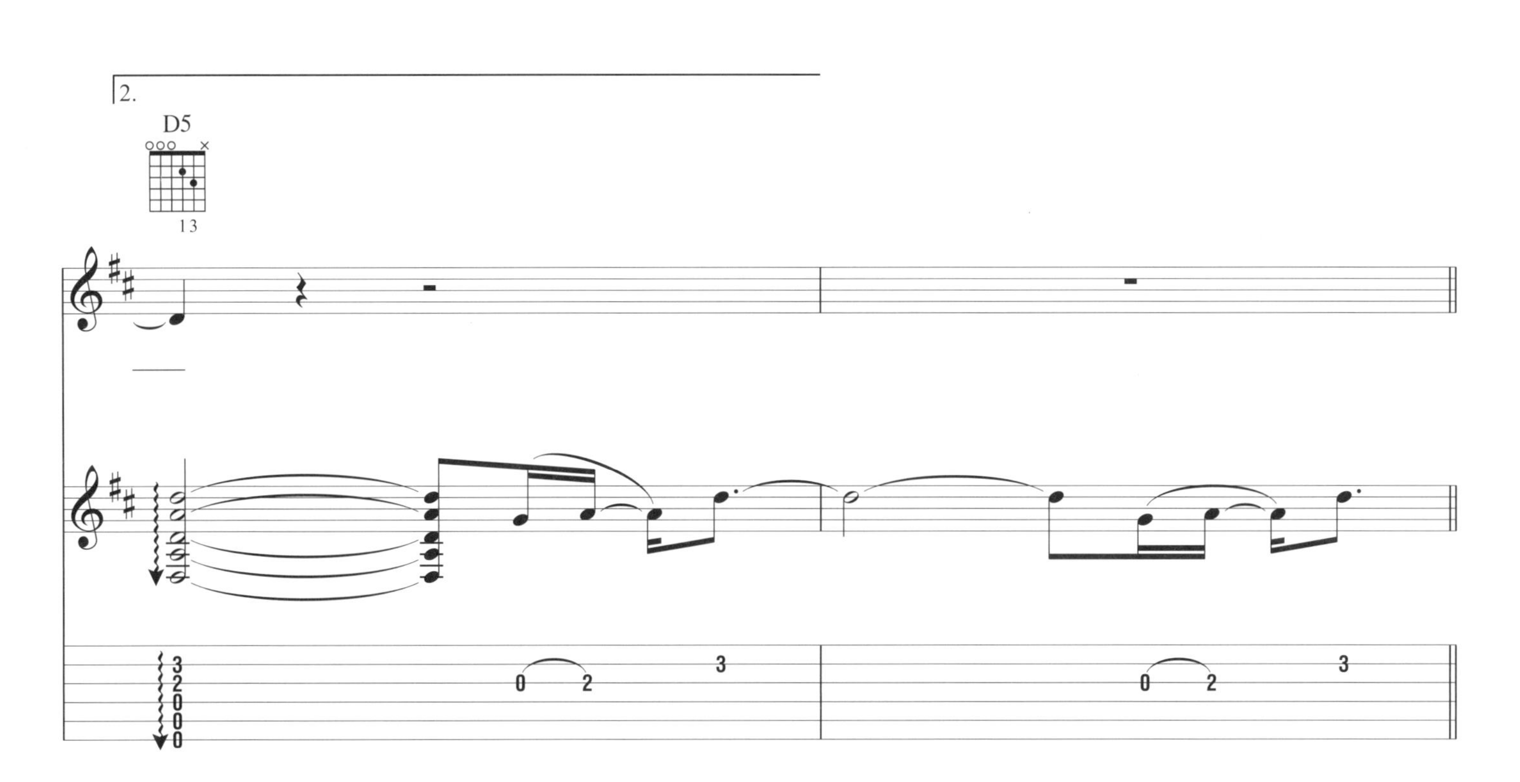
2.
D5

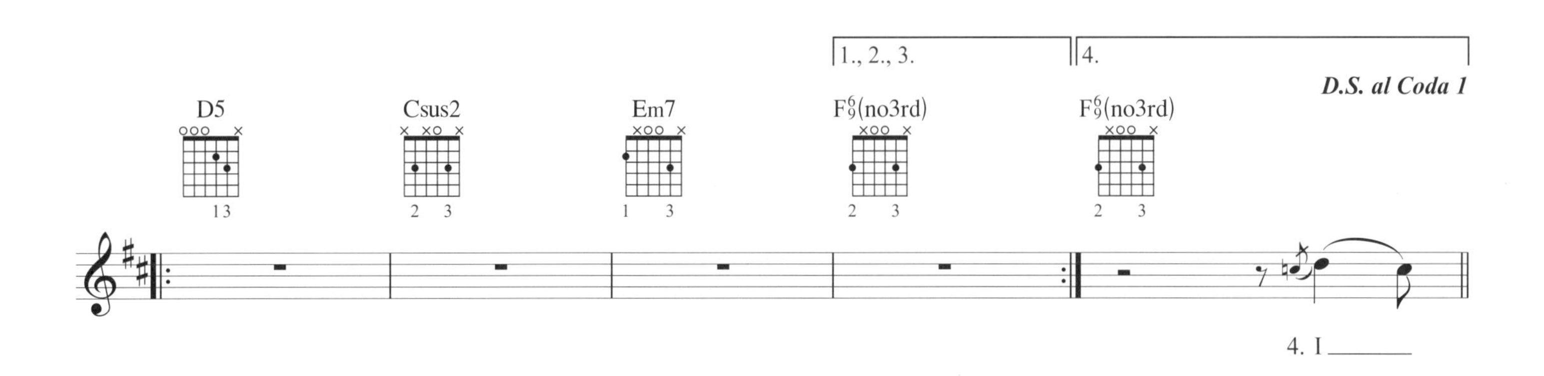
1., 2., 3.
4.
D.S. al Coda 1
D5
Csus2
Em7
F6/9(no3rd)
F6/9(no3rd)
4. I ___

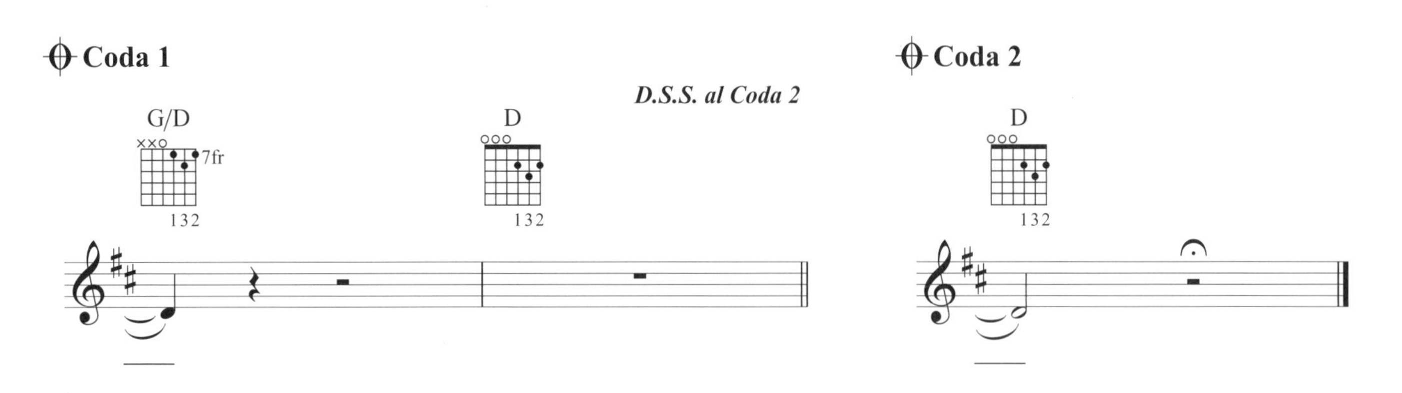
Coda 1
D.S.S. al Coda 2
G/D
7fr
D
Coda 2
D

Letter To The Past

Words and Music by Brandi Marie Carlile, Phillip John Hanseroth and Timothy Jay Hanseroth

F♯m
E
D
hold your breath like that. Ba - by, let it go. You're gon - na
need to know the truth, I still have - n't got a clue. If the
F♯m
E
G
5
feel it in your back. Be - lieve me, I ought - a know.
blind can lead the blind, then ba - by I'm just like you.
You're a stone
Chorus
A
E
wall in a world full of rub - ber bands. You're a
F♯m
E
D
pil - lar of be - lief, still bit - ing your shak - ing / emp - ty hands. Folks are gon - na lean
A
E
on you and leave when the cracks ap - pear, but dar - ling I'll be
F♯m
E
D
Dm
here. I'll be the last. You're my let - ter to the past.

1.
A
G
D
A
2. You can cry.
2.
Interlude
F#m
E
D
F#m
E
G5
D/F#
You're a stone
Chorus
A
E
wall in a world full of rub - ber bands.
You're a

F♯m E D
134111 231 132
pil - lar of be - lief, still hid - ing your emp - ty hands. Folks are gon - na lean
A E C♯/E♯
123 231 14
on you and leave when the cracks ap - pear. Dar - ling, I will
F♯m E B/D♯ D Dm
134111 231 3111 4fr 132 231
be here, I'll be the last. You're my let - ter to the past.
Interlude
A G D A G D A
123 3 132 123 3 132 123
3. It's a game.
Verse
A D
123 132
You know it's o - kay to lose a game, but al - ways re - mem - ber your
A A/G♯ F♯m G D
123 3 111 134111 3 132
rit.
name and have no shame be - cause you're built to last.

Mama Werewolf

Words and Music by Brandi Marie Carlile, Phillip John Hanseroth and Timothy Jay Hanseroth

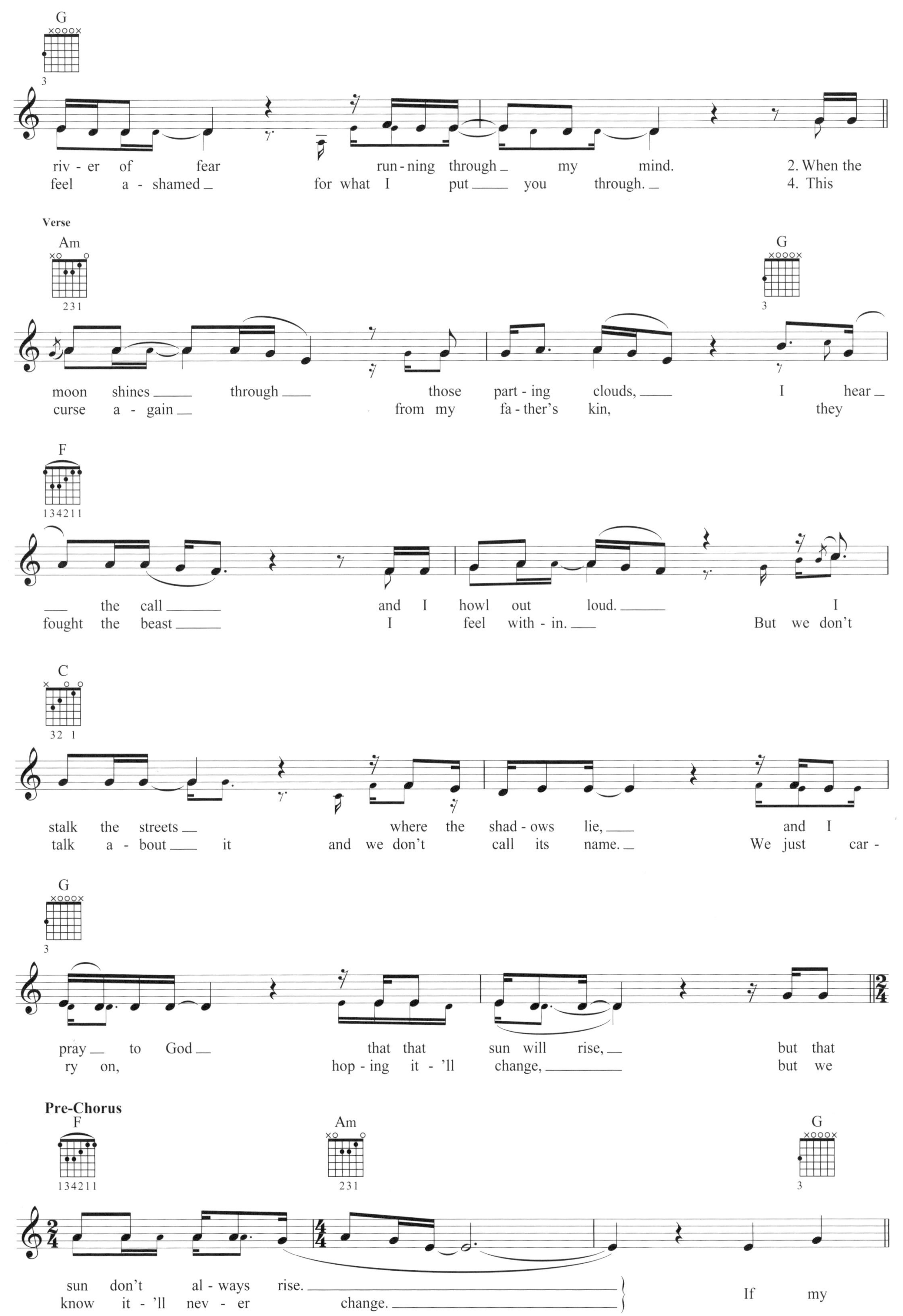
G
riv - er of fear run - ning through my mind. 2. When the
feel a - shamed for what I put you through. 4. This
Verse
Am
G
moon shines through those part - ing clouds, I hear
curse a - gain from my fa - ther's kin, they
F
the call and I howl out loud. I
fought the beast I feel with - in. But we don't
C
stalk the streets where the shad - ows lie, and I
talk a - bout it and we don't call its name. We just car -
G
pray to God that that sun will rise, but that
ry on, hop - ing it - 'll change, but we
Pre-Chorus
F
Am
G
sun don't al - ways rise.
know it - 'll nev - er change.
If my

Chorus
F
C
Am
good in - ten - tions go run - ning wild, if I cause you pain, my

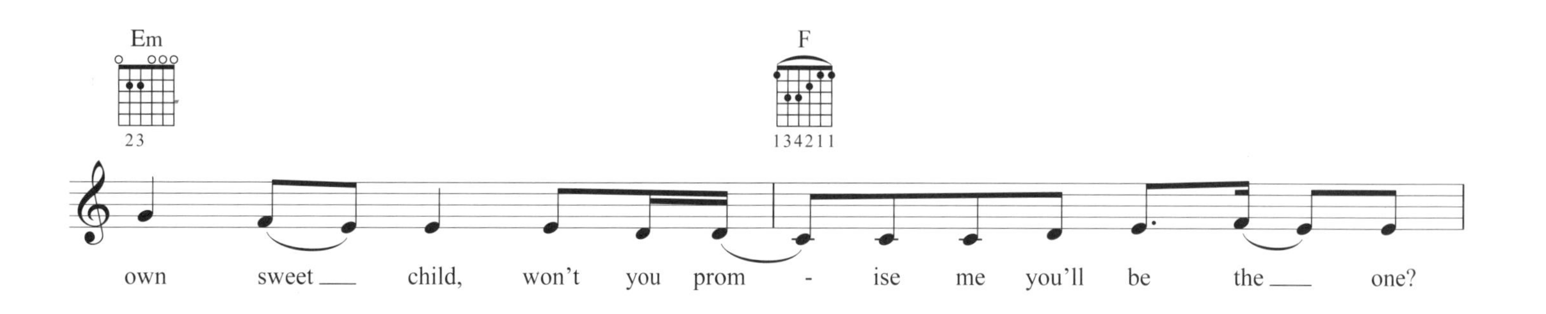
Em
F
own sweet child, won't you prom - ise me you'll be the one?

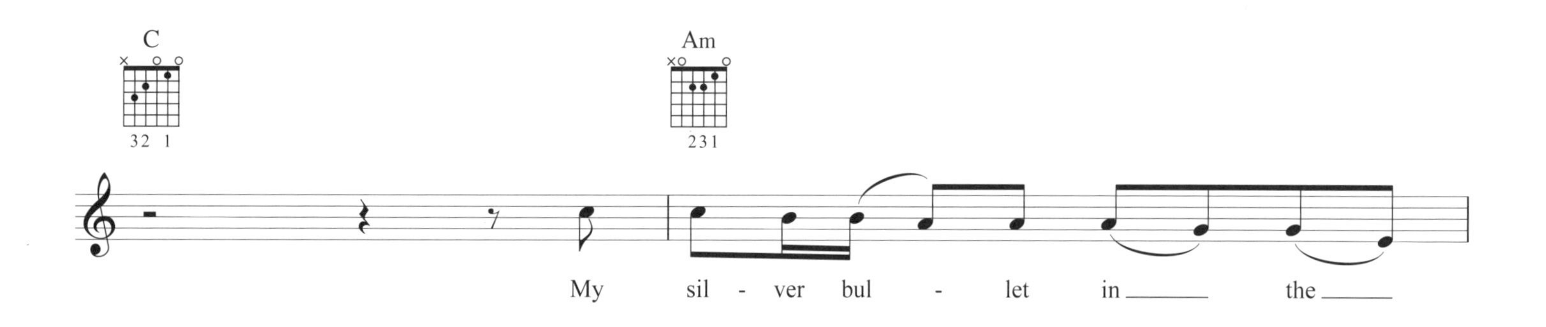
C
Am
My sil - ver bul - let in the

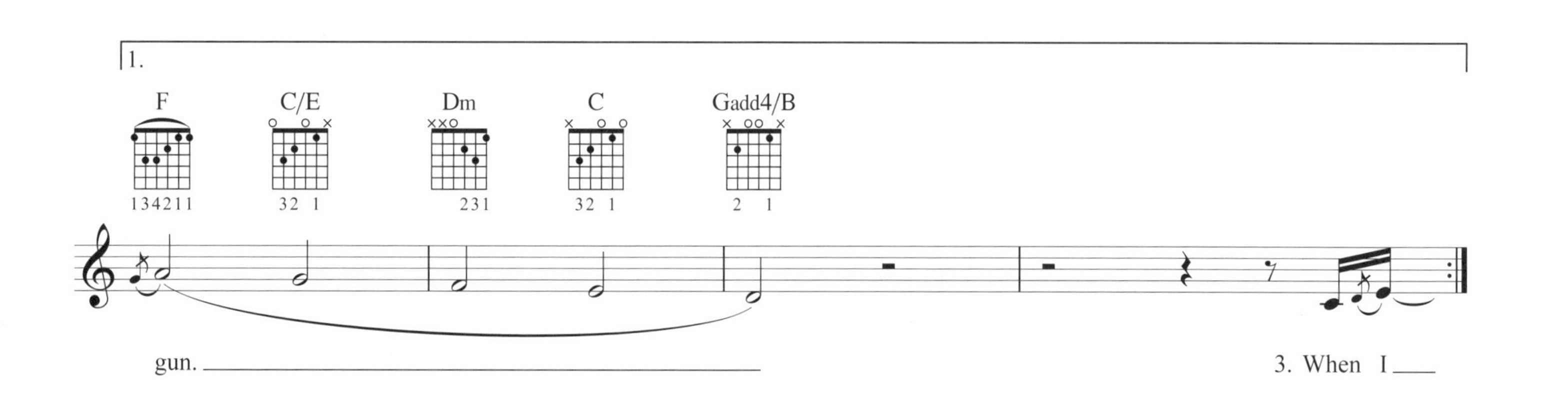
1.
F
C/E
Dm
C
Gadd4/B
gun.
3. When I

2.
Em
F
C
gun. Would you strike me down right where I stand? Would you

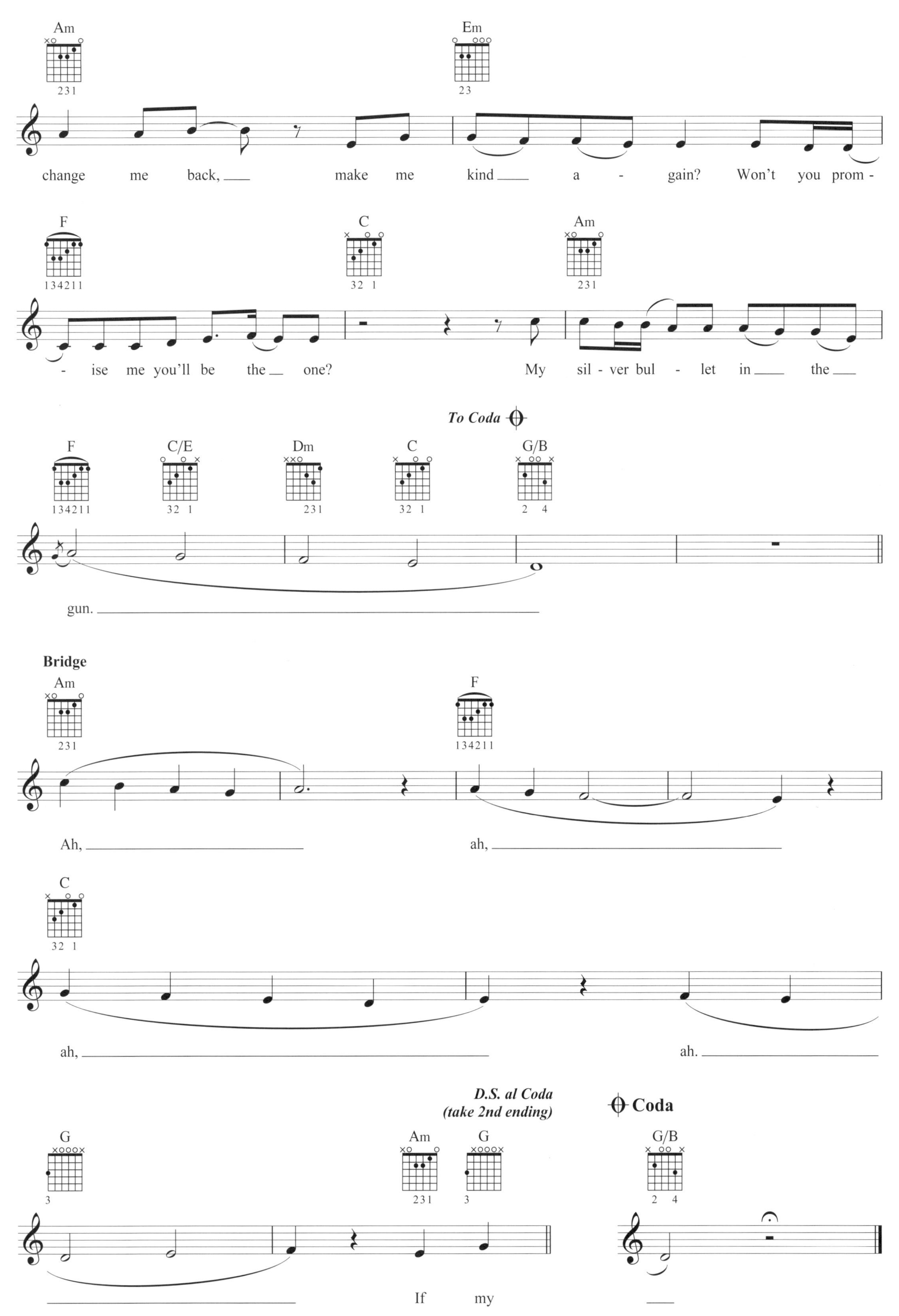
Am
231
Em
23
change me back, make me kind a - gain? Won't you prom -
F
134211
C
32 1
Am
231
- ise me you'll be the one? My sil - ver bul - let in the
To Coda
F
134211
C/E
32 1
Dm
231
C
32 1
G/B
2 4
gun.
Bridge
Am
231
F
134211
Ah,
ah,
C
32 1
ah,
ah.
D.S. al Coda
(take 2nd ending)
Coda
G
3
Am
231
G
3
G/B
2 4
If my

When You're Wrong

Words and Music by Brandi Marie Carlile, Phillip John Hanseroth and Timothy Jay Hanseroth

Verse
Dm
Csus2
creas - es on your fore - head run like treads on a tire. The
day is wind - ing down, my heart a - ban - dons me for you. You for -
G/B
Gm/B♭
white stripe run - ning through your bangs, a long twist - ed spire. You're
got your - self so long a - go, and I wish I could, too. But you
Dm
Csus2
sweep - ing up the floods and you've been vac - uum - ing the fires, and you
live in - side a qui - et hell no one can pray a - way.
G/B
Gm/B♭
Am7
lay down ev - er - y night next to a god - damn li - ar.
Leav - ing would be eas - y, I un - der - stand why you stay.
You
Chorus
Dm
Csus2
may be here to - day, but to - mor - row you're a ghost. I guess the most
G/B
Gm/B♭
some - one can hope for is to find a place to lay. Some -

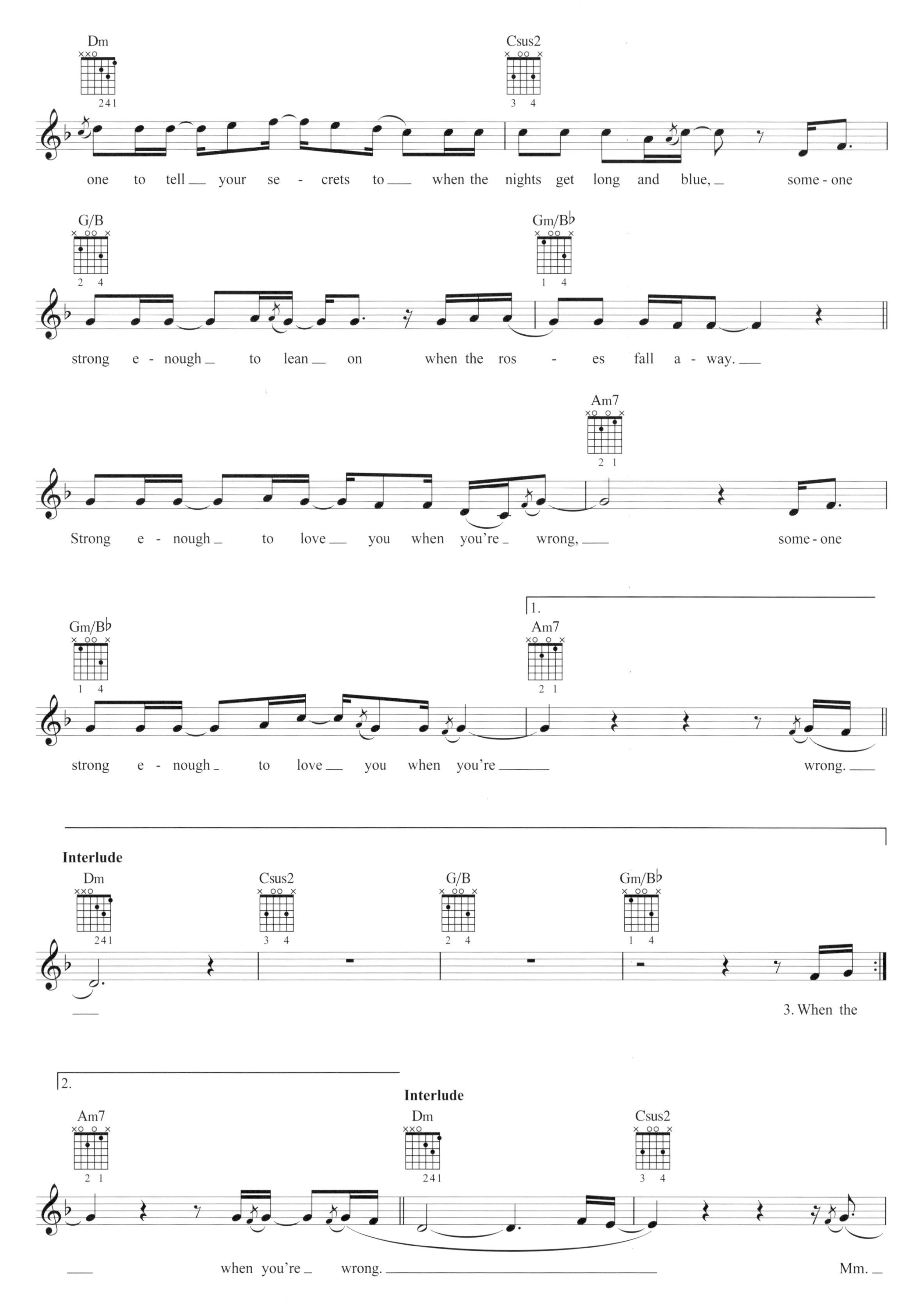
Dm
Csus2
one to tell your se - crets to when the nights get long and blue, some - one
G/B
Gm/B♭
strong e - nough to lean on when the ros - es fall a - way.
Am7
Strong e - nough to love you when you're wrong, some - one
Gm/B♭
1.
Am7
strong e - nough to love you when you're wrong.
Interlude
Dm
Csus2
G/B
Gm/B♭
3. When the
2.
Am7
Interlude
Dm
Csus2
when you're wrong. Mm.

G/B
Gm/B♭
4. You'll be wrong
Verse
Dm
Csus2
if you were think - ing that we all don't fade a - way like
G/B
Gm/B♭
dew - drops in the dawn, like sun - beams through the haze. It's a long
Dm
Csus2
way to be sink - ing, hold - ing tight - ly to the weight of the
G/B
Gm/B♭
one who pulls you down while you slow - ly waste your days.
Am7
Gm/B♭
Some - one strong e - nough to love you when you're wrong,
Am7
Gm/B♭
Am7
some - one strong e - nough to love you when you're wrong,

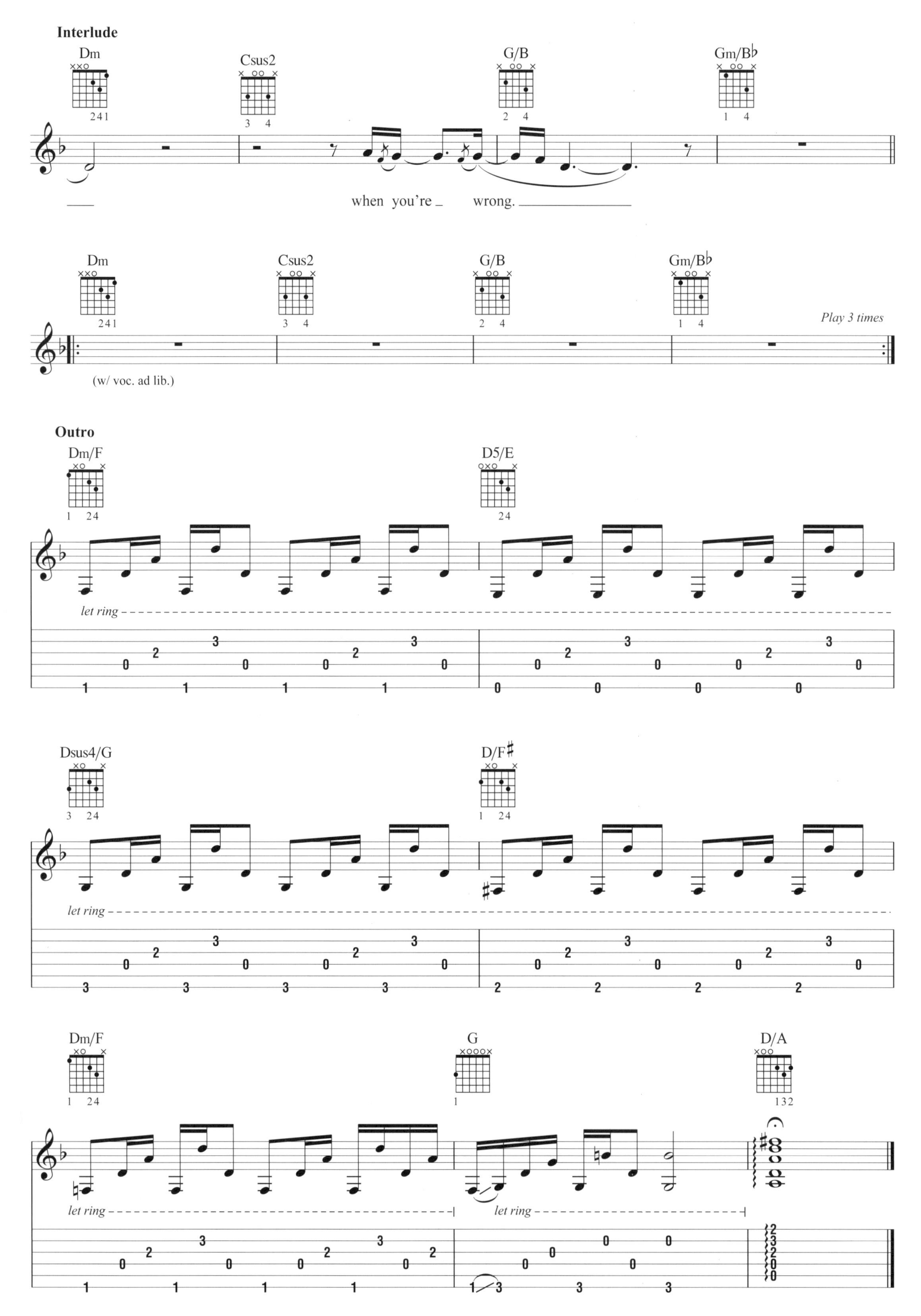
Interlude
Dm
Csus2
G/B
Gm/B♭
when you're wrong.
(w/ voc. ad lib.)
Play 3 times
Outro
Dm/F
D5/E
let ring
Dsus4/G
D/F♯
G
D/A

Stay Gentle

Words and Music by Brandi Marie Carlile, Phillip John Hanseroth and Timothy Jay Hanseroth

Am7
D7
D7/F♯
though they will think you don't un - der - stand.
think you are na - ive.
G
G/F♯
Em
Am7
D7
Don't let the world make you cal - lous. Be read - y to laugh.
Don't let them low - er your shoul - ders. Love them more while they try. Grow
G
G/F♯
Em
Am
D7
No one's for - got - ten a - bout us. There is light on your path.
young - er while you're grow - ing old - er. Be a - mazed by the sky.
Bridge
D7/F♯
Em
Bm
Dar - ling, stay wild if you can. The
C
G
D/F♯
girl with the world in her hands. The
Em
Bm
king - dom of heav - en be - longs to a boy while his

Am
D7
D7/F♯
wor - ry be - longs to a man.
Verse
G
Am
B7
Em
3. Stay gen - tle, stay gen - tle, the most
C
Dadd4
Em
pow - er - ful thing you can do.
Am
D7
Oh, gen - tle un - break - a - ble
Outro
G
Em
Am
D7
G
you.
mf

Sinners, Saints And Fools

Words and Music by Brandi Marie Carlile, Phillip John Hanseroth and Timothy Jay Hanseroth

Capo VIII

Intro
Moderately slow ♩ = 75

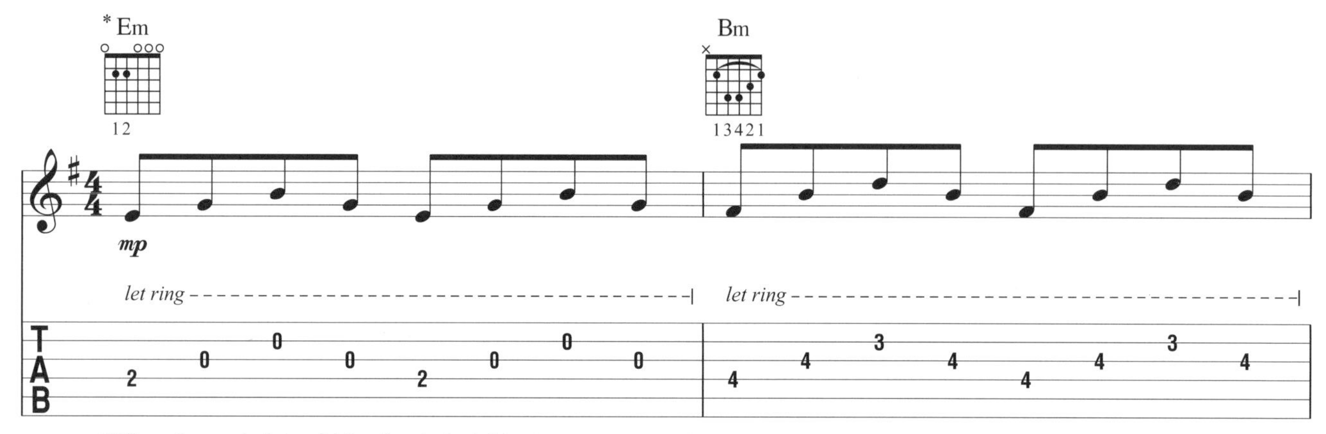

*All music sounds 4 steps higher than indicated due to capo.
Vocals are written one octave higher.

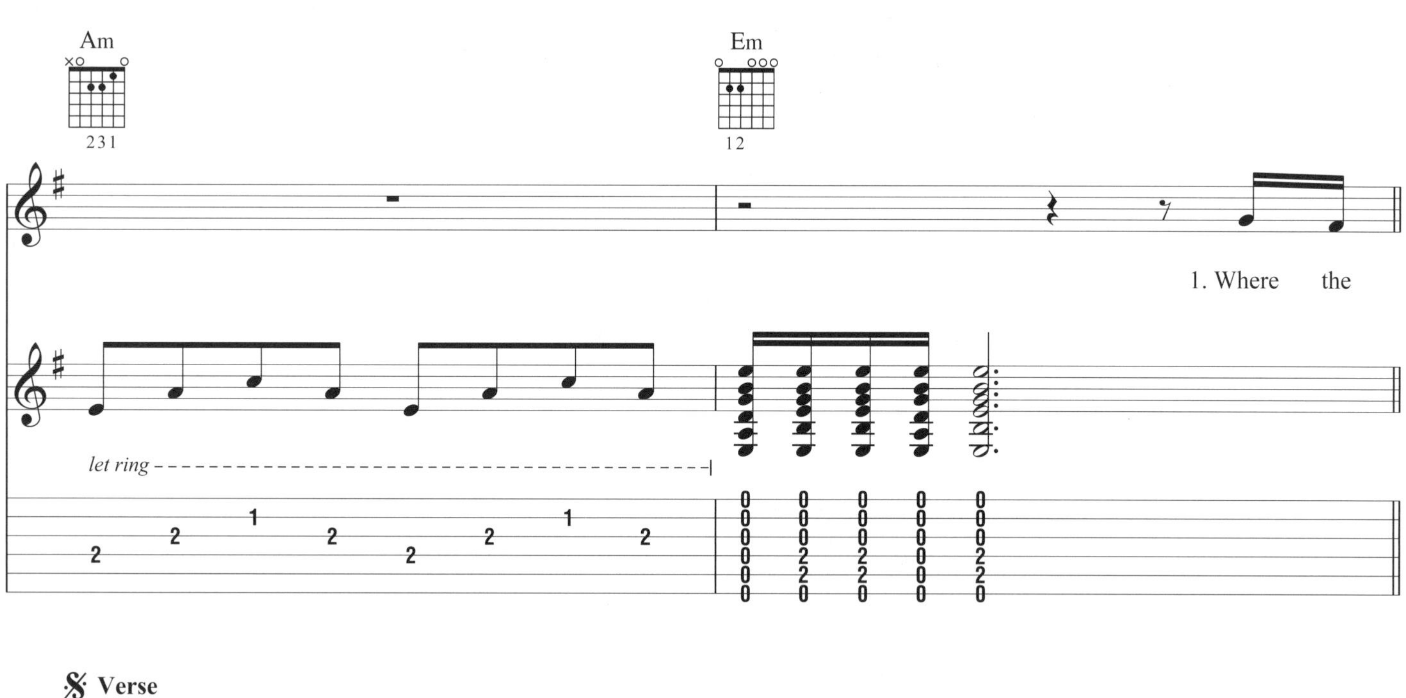

Verse

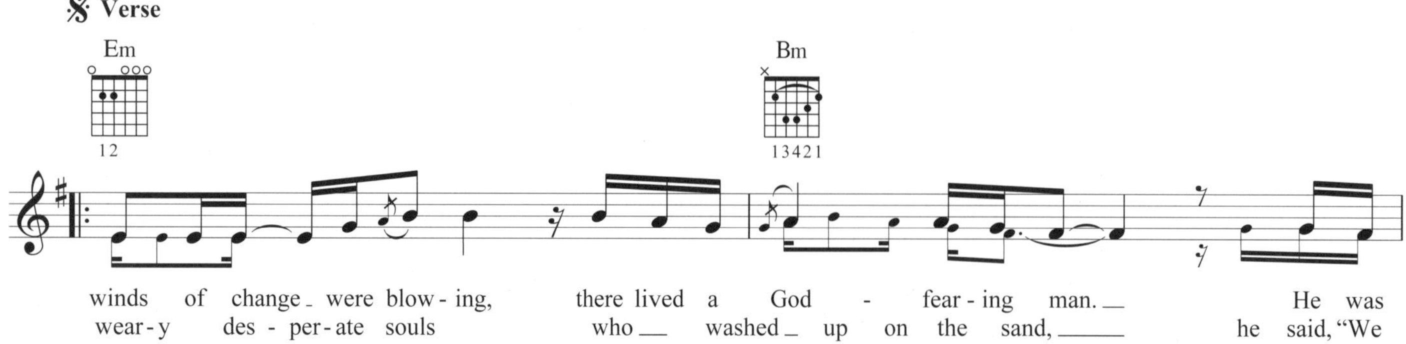

Am
231
D
132
Em
12
turn-ing through his Bi - ble, when he came up with a plan. He
have-n't seen your pa - per work," and he with - drew his hand. You know he

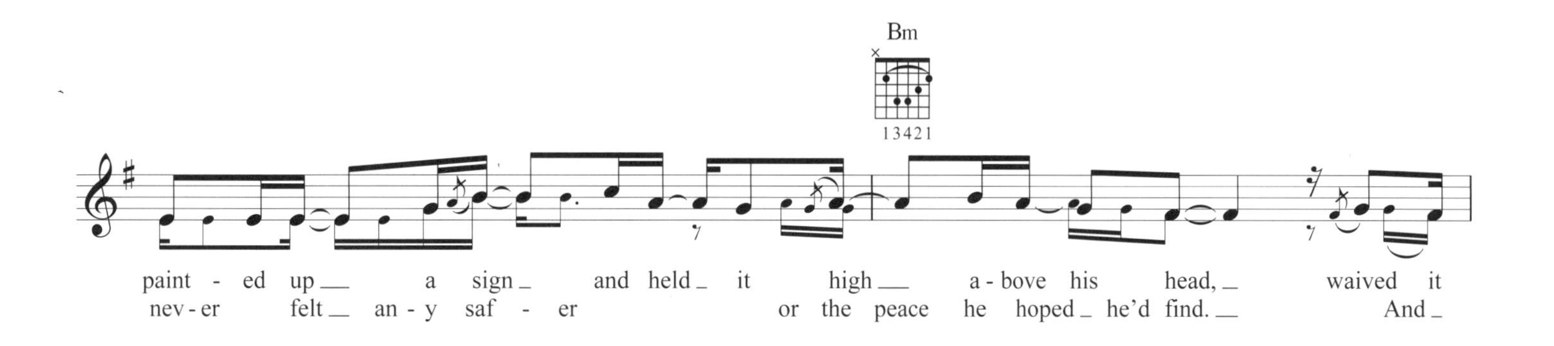
Bm
13421
paint - ed up a sign and held it high a - bove his head, waived it
nev-er felt an-y saf - er or the peace he hoped he'd find. And

Am
231
D
132
Em
12
D/F♯
1 23
proud - ly in the air, and this is what it read:
up un - til the day he died, he nev-er changed his mind.

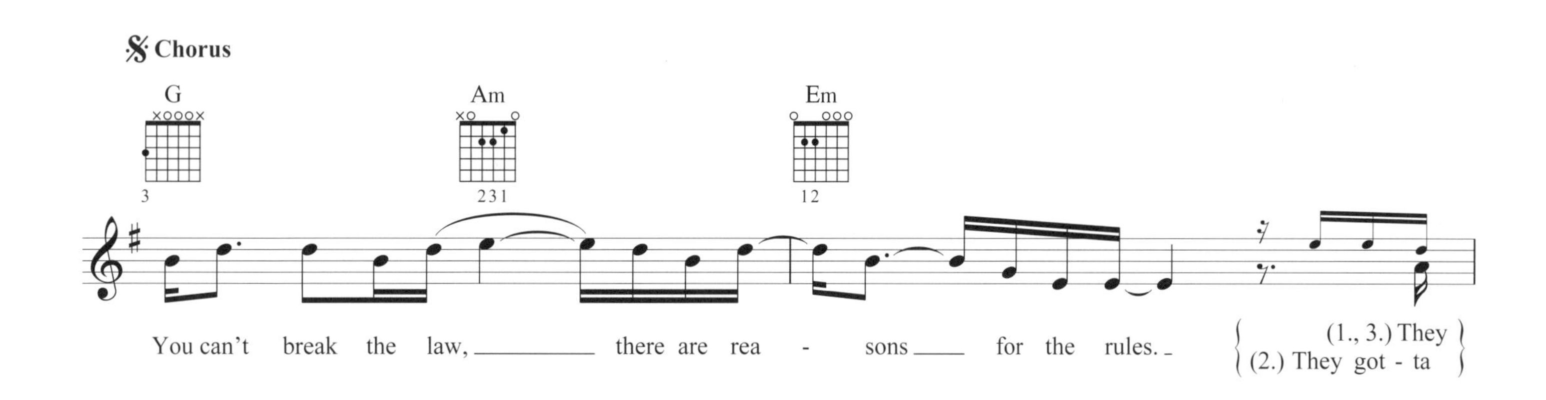
Chorus
G
3
Am
231
Em
12
You can't break the law, there are rea - sons for the rules. (1., 3.) They (2.) They got - ta

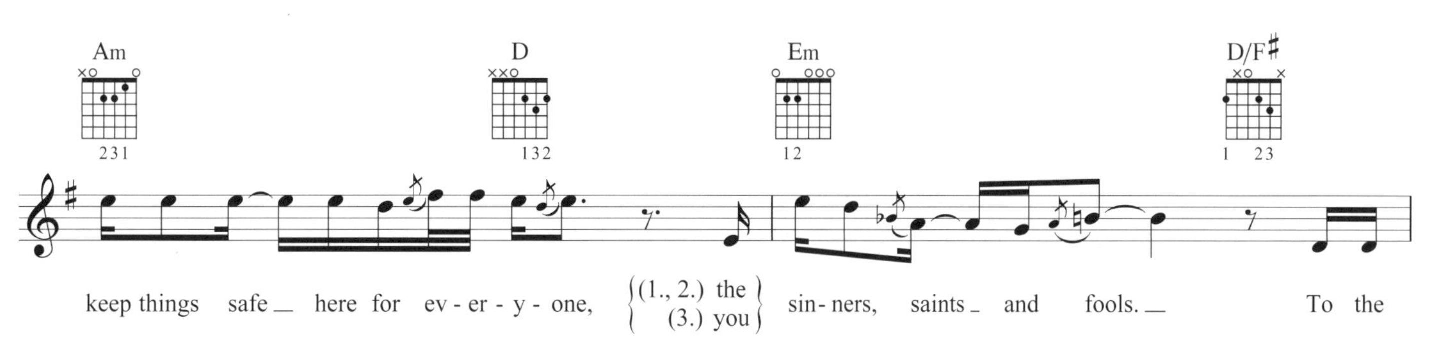
Am
231
D
132
Em
12
D/F♯
1 23
keep things safe here for ev-er-y-one, (1., 2.) the (3.) you sin-ners, saints and fools. To the

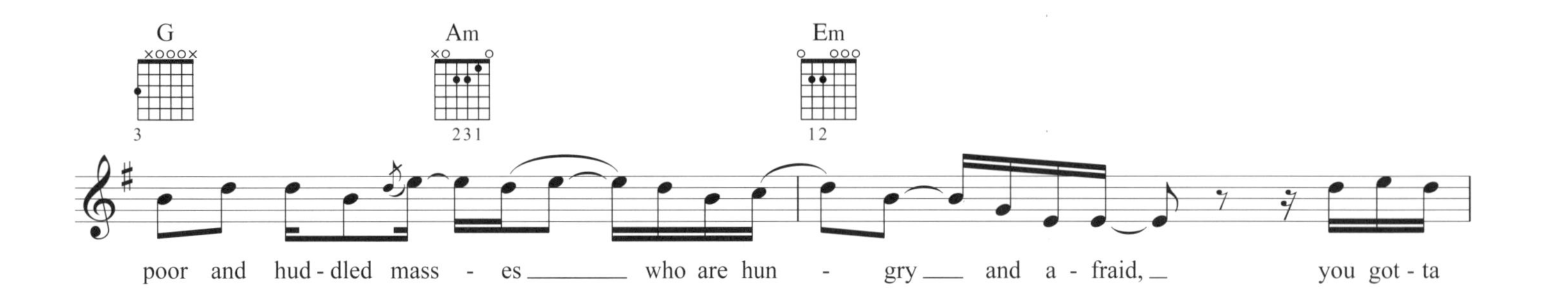
G
3
Am
231
Em
12
poor and hud-dled mass - es who are hun - gry and a - fraid, you got - ta

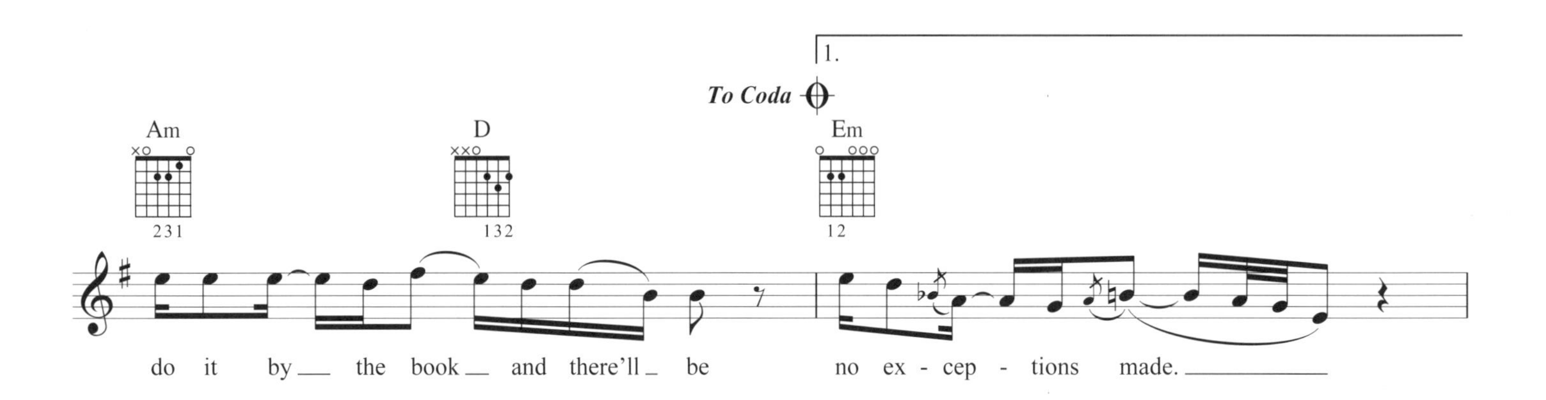
1.
To Coda
Am
231
D
132
Em
12
do it by the book and there'll be no ex - cep - tions made.

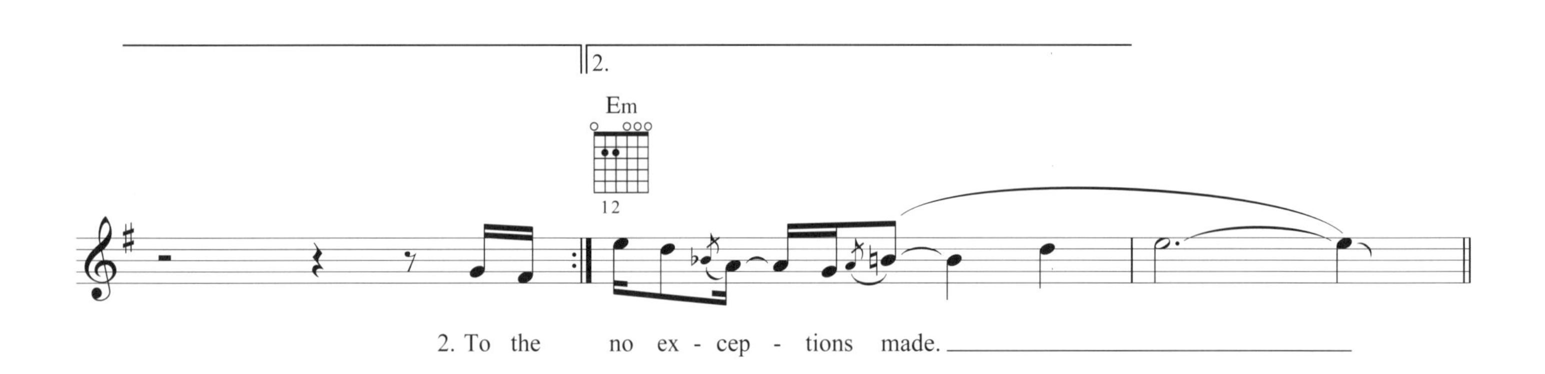
2.
Em
12
2. To the no ex - cep - tions made.

Interlude

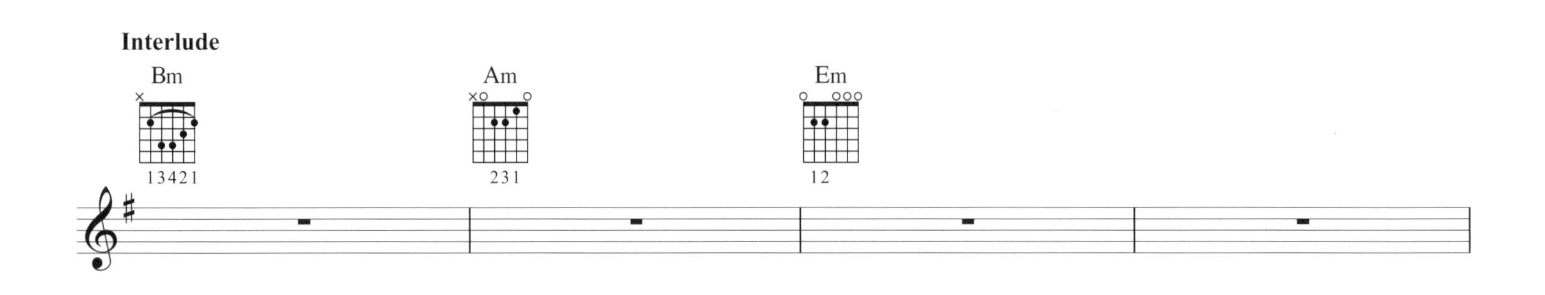
Bm
13421
Am
231
Em
12

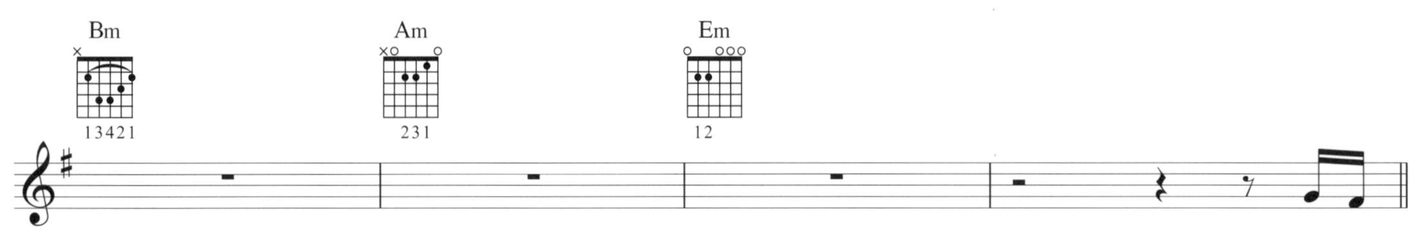
Bm
13421
Am
231
Em
12
3. By the

Verse
Em
Bm
12
13421
time he got to heav - en,
it was sur - round - ed by a wall.
The

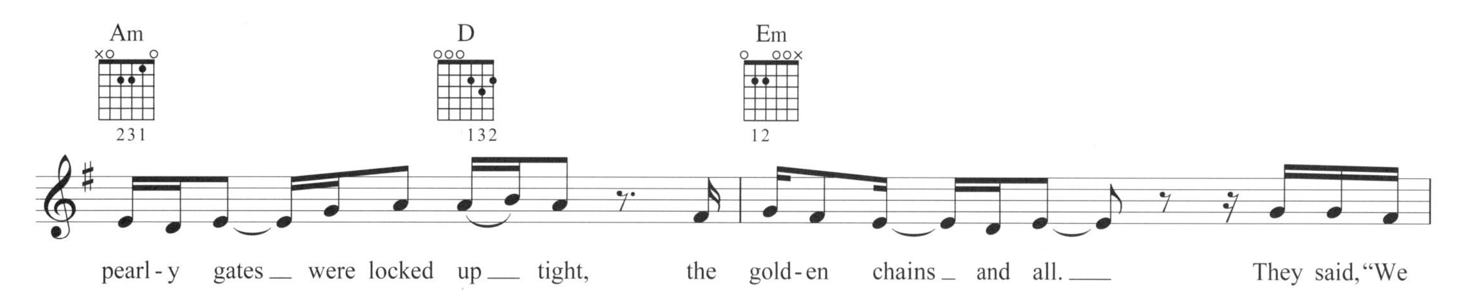
Am
D
Em
231
132
12
pearl - y gates were locked up tight,
the gold - en chains and all.
They said, "We

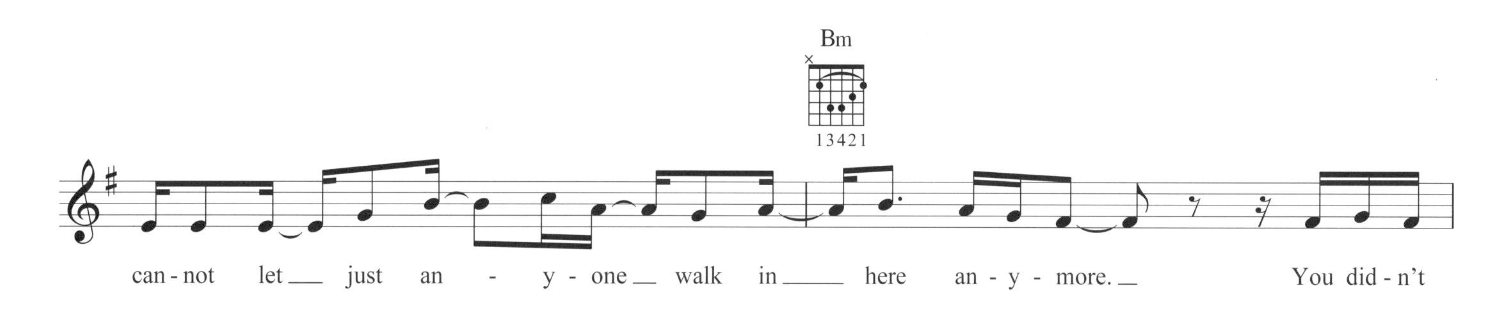
Bm
13421
can - not let just an - y - one walk in here an - y - more.
You did - n't

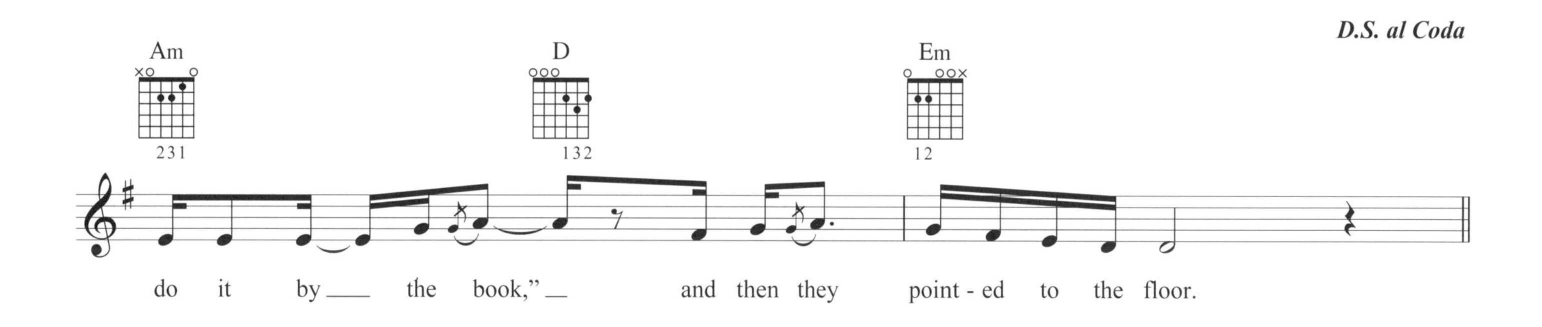
D.S. al Coda
Am
D
Em
231
132
12
do it by the book,"
and then they point - ed to the floor.

Coda

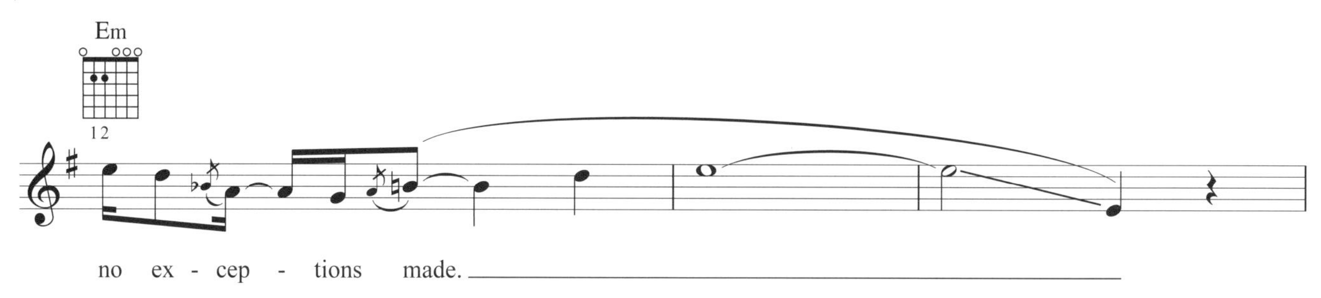
Em
12
no ex - cep - tions made.

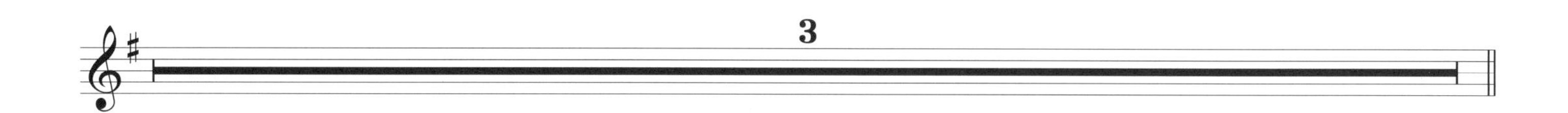
3

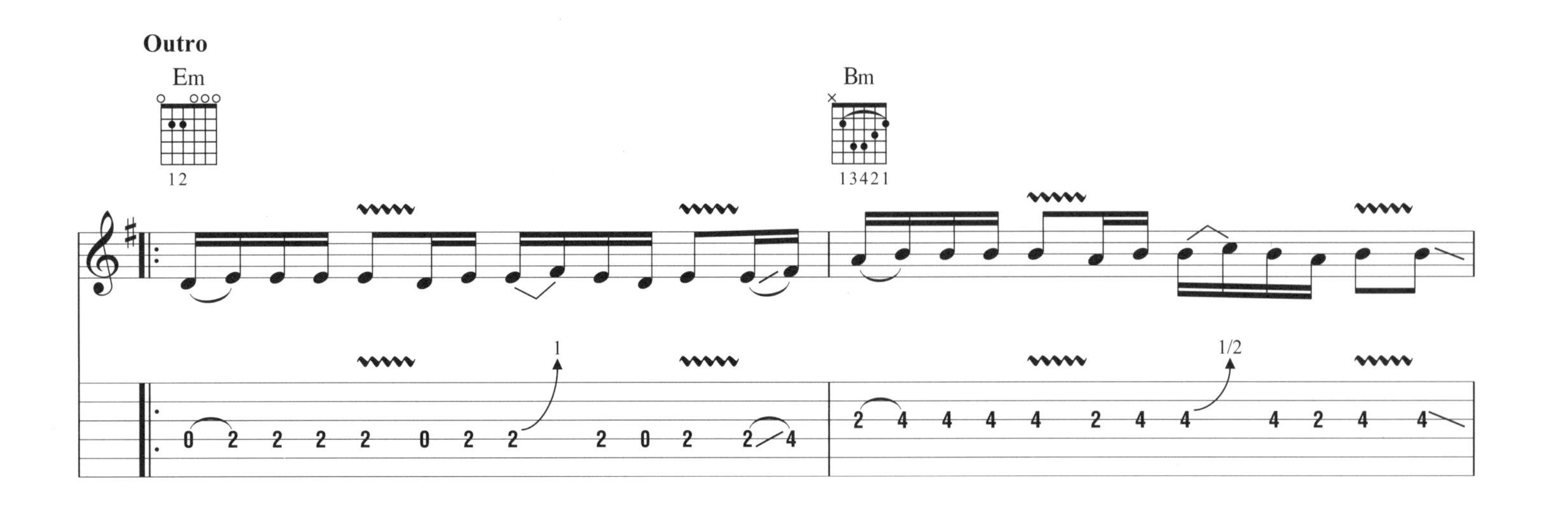
Outro
Em
Bm

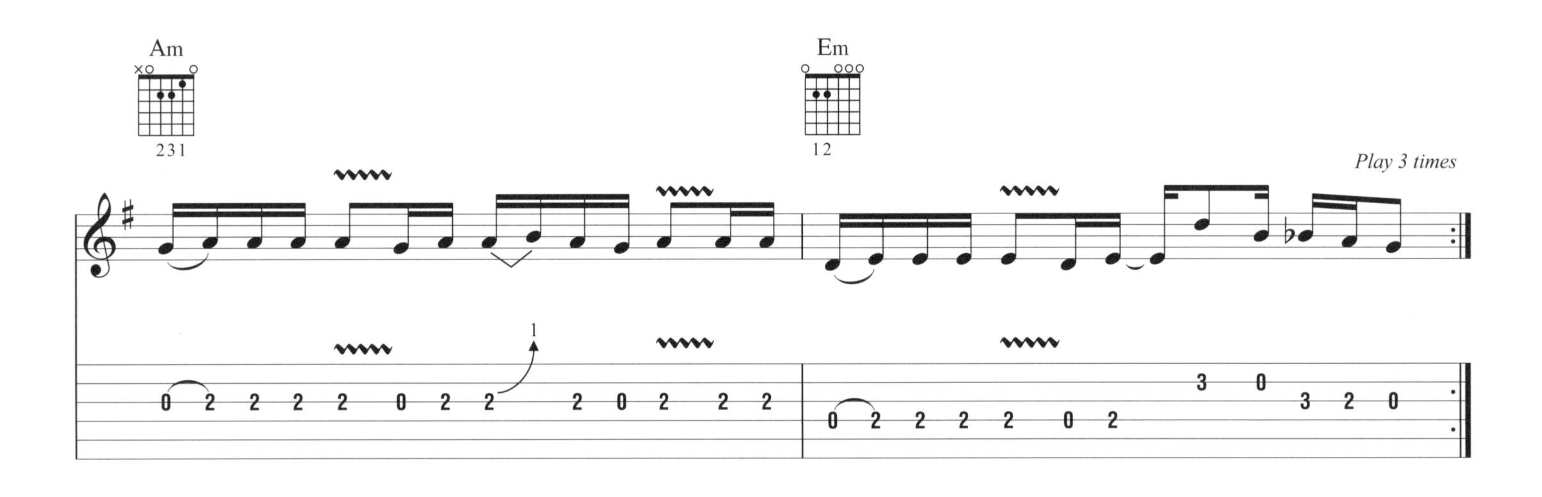
Am
Em
Play 3 times

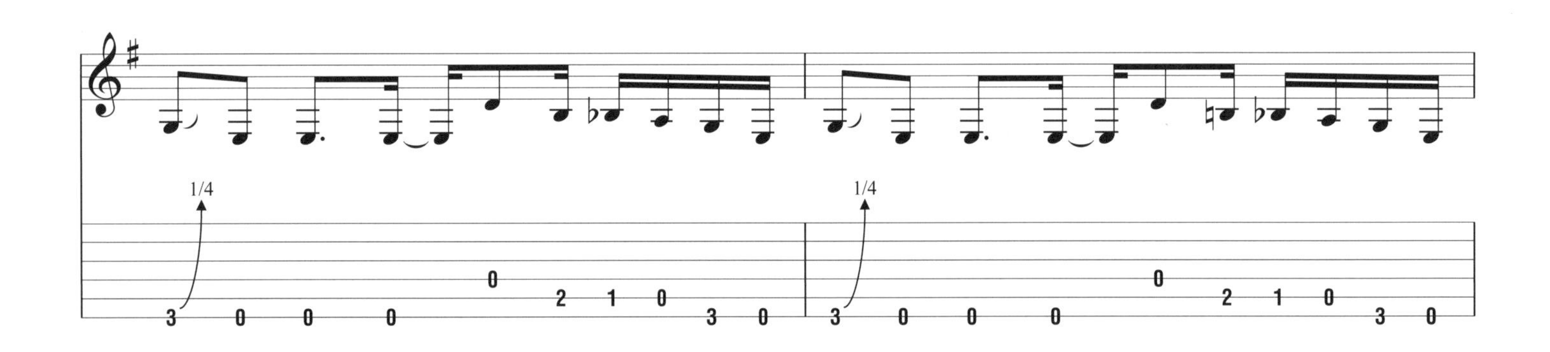

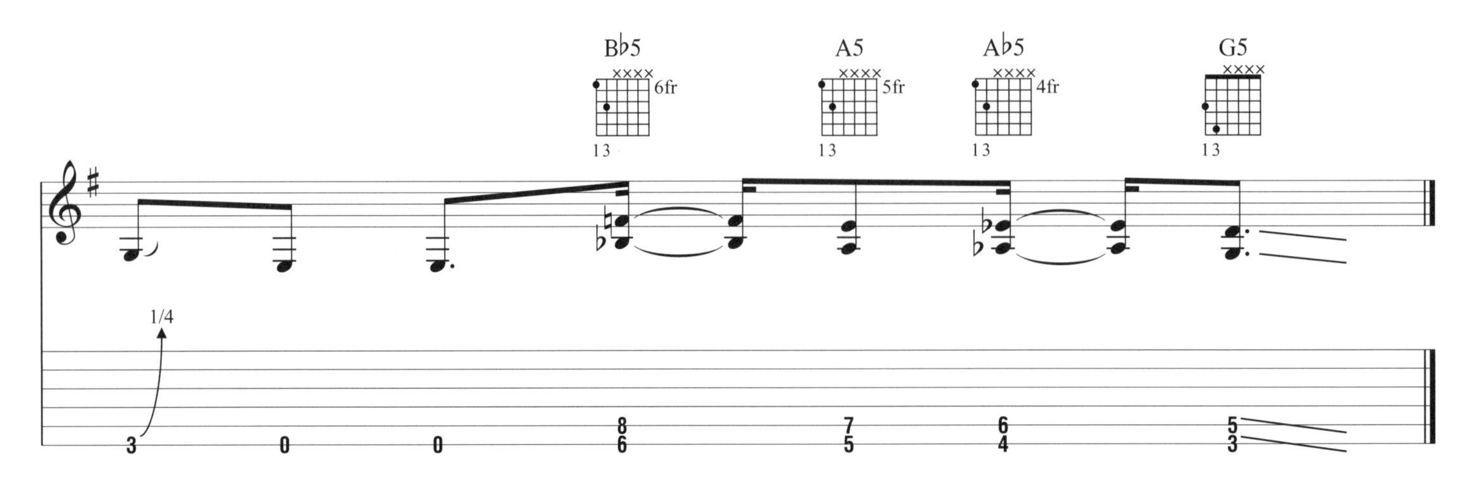
B♭5
6fr
A5
5fr
A♭5
4fr
G5

Throwing Good After Bad

Words and Music by Brandi Marie Carlile, Phillip John Hanseroth and Timothy Jay Hanseroth

G
3
D
132
ie danc - er, you want blood from a stone. But I'm on
all that cha - os will lead to some-thing like this. I'll get o -
Bm
13421
F♯m
134111
3
to you, and you will pour your heart in - to an - y shim-mer - ing fad,
- ver you, but you won't be whole un - til you do. You won't find what you
1.
G
A
111
D
throw - ing good af - ter bad. 2. Peo - ple get ad - dict - ed
had, throw - ing good af - ter
2.
Pre-Chorus
D/F♯
1 23
bad. And I'll al - ways feel a lit - tle left be - hind.
F♯
134211
But that ly - ing wind that calls your name will
E
231
E7
2314
leave you fly - ing blind. Are you

Chorus
G D/F# D F#m
fan - ta - siz - ing? You're tak - ing us for grant - ed. I know you are bored.
G A
You al - ways say I'm heav - y hand - ed. You got a
G D/F# D G D/F# D
beau - ti - ful mind and the soul of a coy - o - te. Hun - ger driv - ing you mad,
To Coda
G A D
throw - ing good af - ter bad. Hun - ger driv - ing you mad,
G A G D
throw - ing good af - ter bad. 3. I know you loved
Verse
G D
me once, you were some - thing to prove. I was an un -

G
D
fin - ished song, you were noth - ing to lose. I'm a dan -
Bm
F♯m
- de - li - on and when my col - or suit - ed you, you al - lowed me to grow.
G
E
E7
But you know when you know. And now the par - ty's o -
D
G
ver and you're danc - ing a - lone. You been
Bm
A
E
spin-ning a-round for hours (and the) band have all gone home.
E7
D.S. al Coda
Coda
G
D
And you're bad. Hun - ger driv - ing you mad,

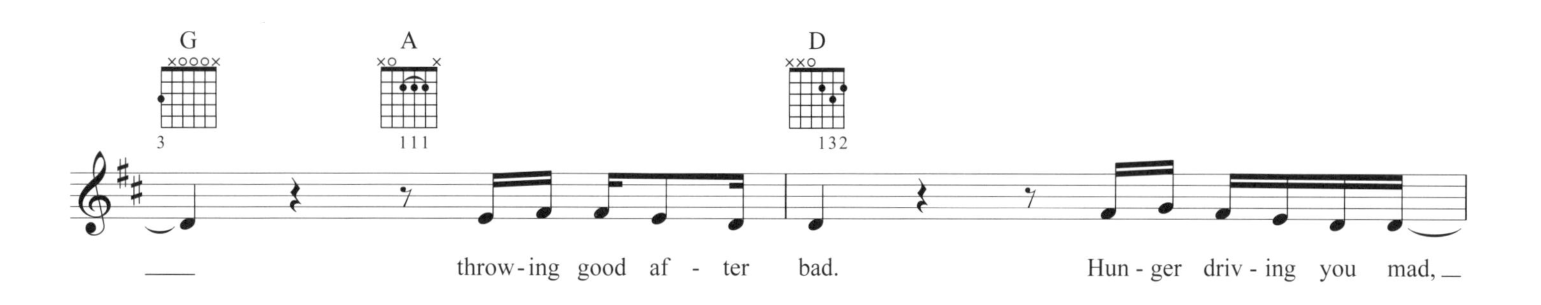
G
A
D
3
111
132
throw-ing good af - ter bad.
Hun-ger driv-ing you mad,

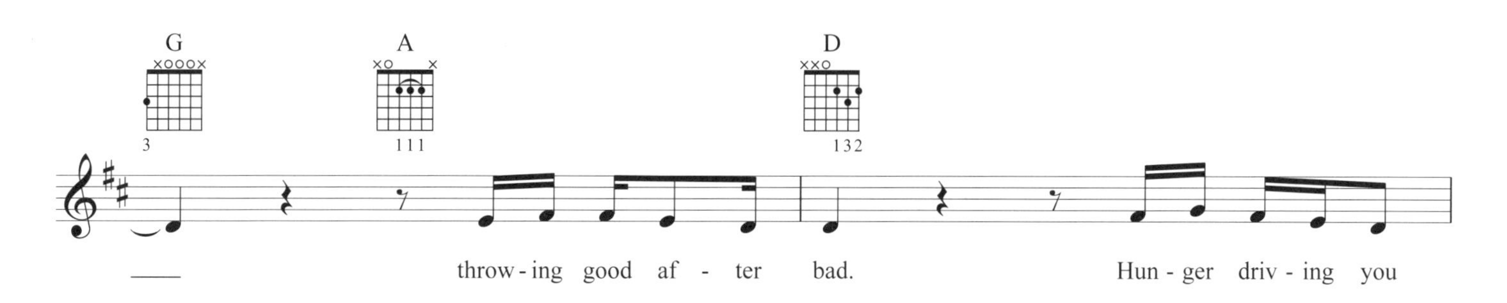
G
A
D
3
111
132
throw-ing good af - ter bad.
Hun-ger driv-ing you

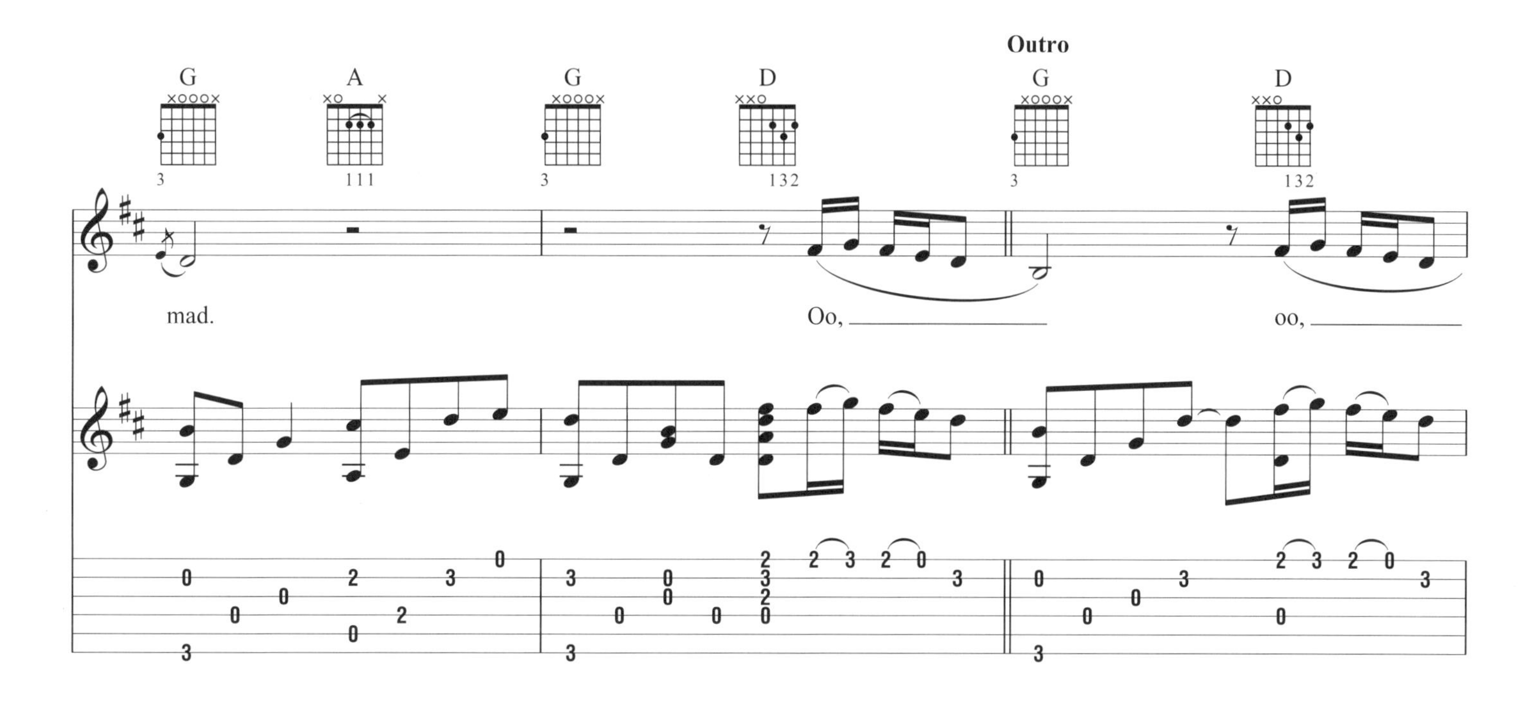
Outro
G
A
G
D
G
D
mad.
Oo,
oo,

G
D
rit.
oo.

GUITAR NOTATION LEGEND

Guitar music can be notated three different ways: on a *musical staff*, in *tablature*, and in *rhythm slashes*.

RHYTHM SLASHES are written above the staff. Strum chords in the rhythm indicated. Use the chord diagrams found at the top of the first page of the transcription for the appropriate chord voicings. Round noteheads indicate single notes.

THE MUSICAL STAFF shows pitches and rhythms and is divided by bar lines into measures. Pitches are named after the first seven letters of the alphabet.

TABLATURE graphically represents the guitar fingerboard. Each horizontal line represents a string, and each number represents a fret.

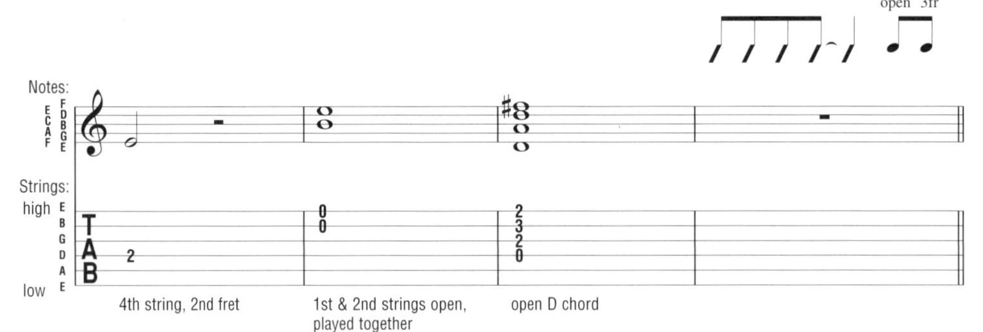

HALF-STEP BEND: Strike the note and bend up 1/2 step.

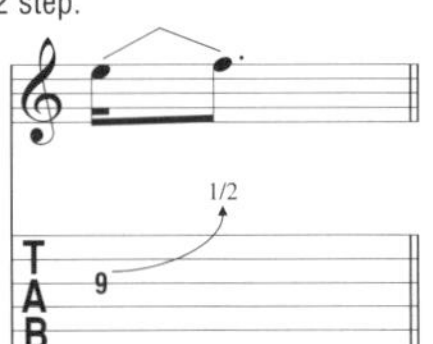

WHOLE-STEP BEND: Strike the note and bend up one step.

GRACE NOTE BEND: Strike the note and immediately bend up as indicated.

SLIGHT (MICROTONE) BEND: Strike the note and bend up 1/4 step.

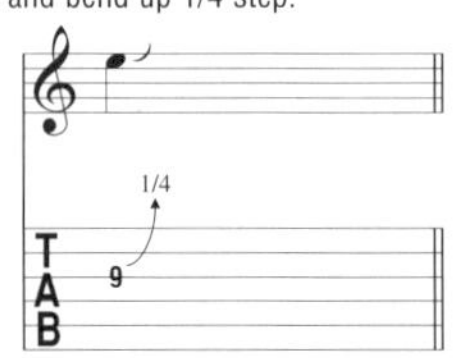

BEND AND RELEASE: Strike the note and bend up as indicated, then release back to the original note. Only the first note is struck.

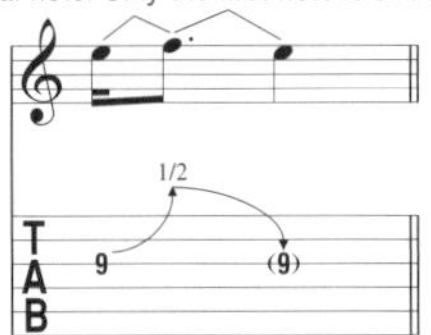

PRE-BEND: Bend the note as indicated, then strike it.

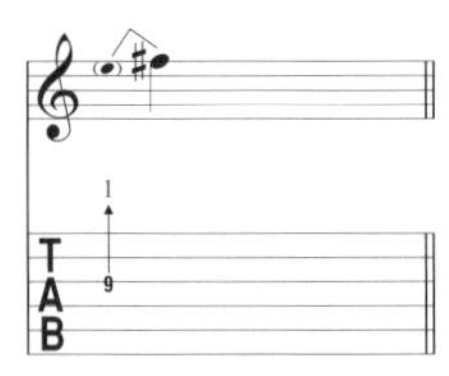

VIBRATO: The string is vibrated by rapidly bending and releasing the note with the fretting hand.

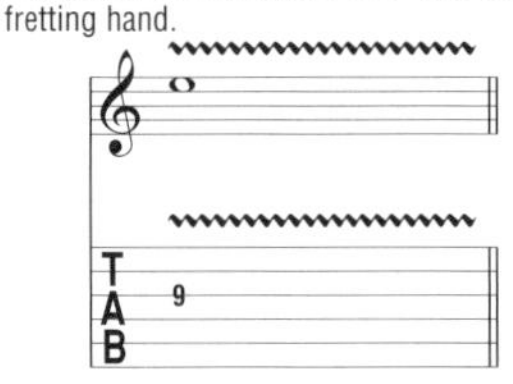

WIDE VIBRATO: The pitch is varied to a greater degree by vibrating with the fretting hand.

HAMMER-ON: Strike the first (lower) note with one finger, then sound the higher note (on the same string) with another finger by fretting it without picking.

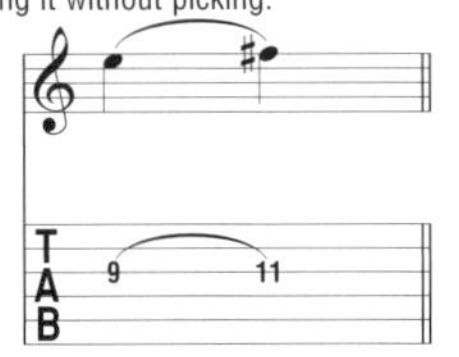

PULL-OFF: Place both fingers on the notes to be sounded. Strike the first note and without picking, pull the finger off to sound the second (lower) note.

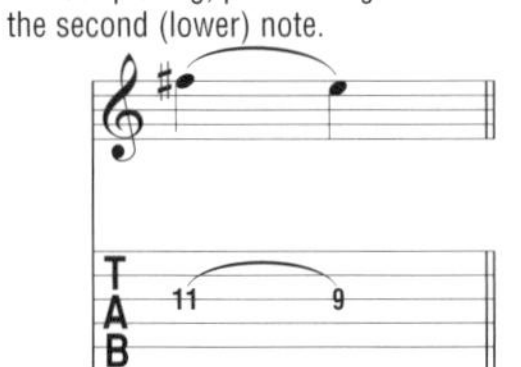

LEGATO SLIDE: Strike the first note and then slide the same fret-hand finger up or down to the second note. The second note is not struck.

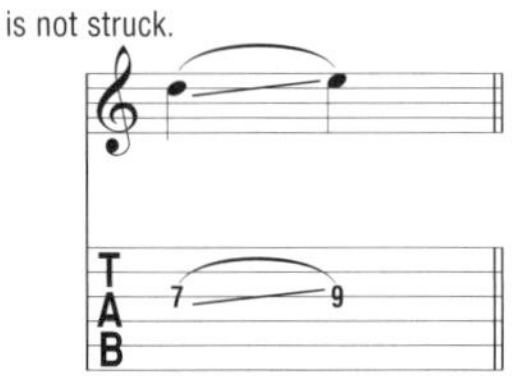

SHIFT SLIDE: Same as legato slide, except the second note is struck.

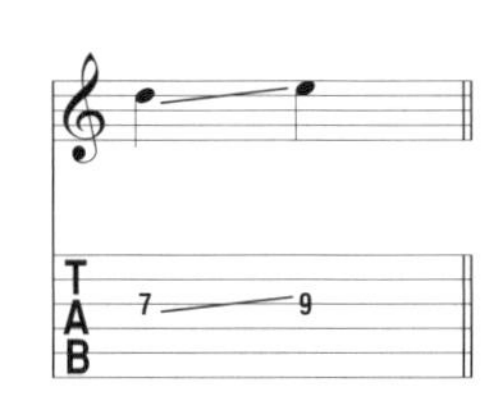

TRILL: Very rapidly alternate between the notes indicated by continuously hammering on and pulling off.

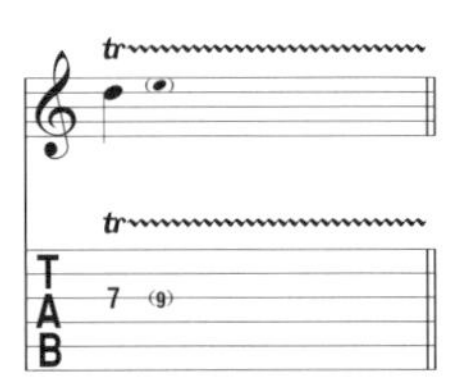

TAPPING: Hammer ("tap") the fret indicated with the pick-hand index or middle finger and pull off to the note fretted by the fret hand.

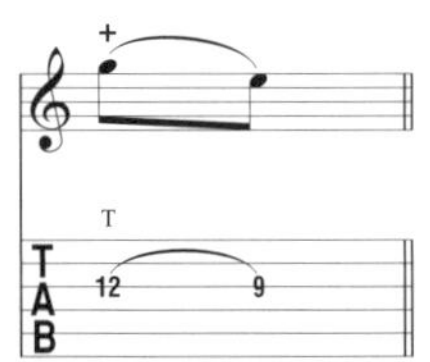

NATURAL HARMONIC: Strike the note while the fret-hand lightly touches the string directly over the fret indicated.

PINCH HARMONIC: The note is fretted normally and a harmonic is produced by adding the edge of the thumb or the tip of the index finger of the pick hand to the normal pick attack.

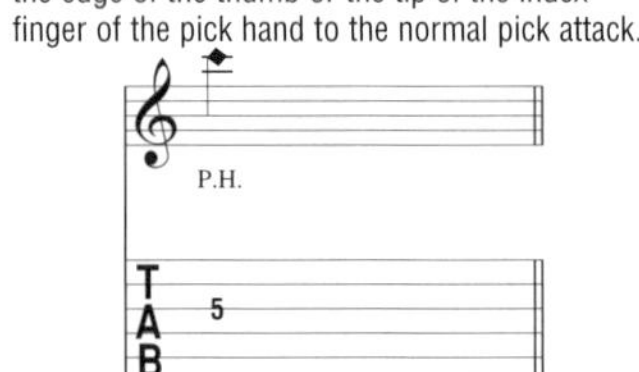

PICK SCRAPE: The edge of the pick is rubbed down (or up) the string, producing a scratchy sound.

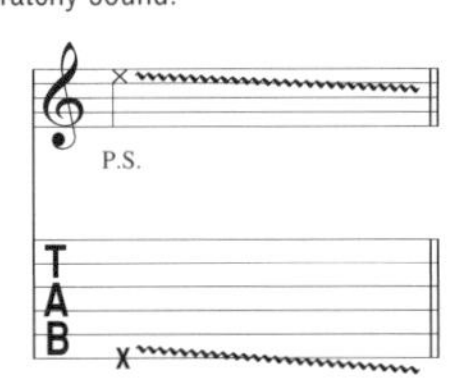

MUFFLED STRINGS: A percussive sound is produced by laying the fret hand across the string(s) without depressing, and striking them with the pick hand.

PALM MUTING: The note is partially muted by the pick hand lightly touching the string(s) just before the bridge.

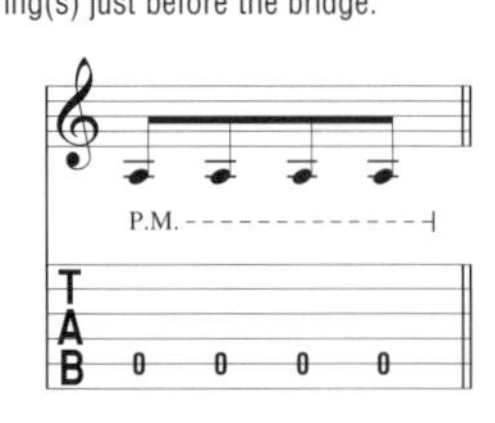

RAKE: Drag the pick across the strings indicated with a single motion.

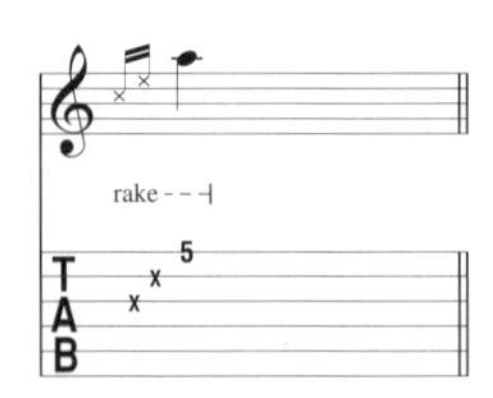

TREMOLO PICKING: The note is picked as rapidly and continuously as possible.

VIBRATO BAR DIVE AND RETURN: The pitch of the note or chord is dropped a specified number of steps (in rhythm), then returned to the original pitch.

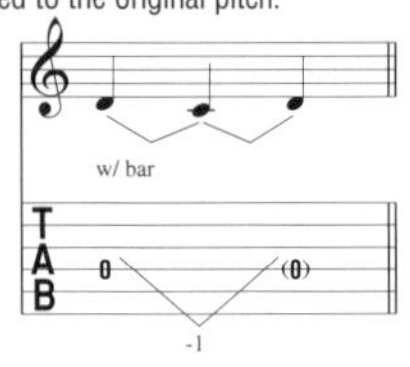

VIBRATO BAR SCOOP: Depress the bar just before striking the note, then quickly release the bar.

VIBRATO BAR DIP: Strike the note and then immediately drop a specified number of steps, then release back to the original pitch.